Pick Yourself For Success: How To Step Out Of Your Head And Into Your Greatness

Copyright © 2024 by Rodney Goldston

All rights reserved. No part of this book may be reproduced by any mechanical, photographic, or electronic process, or in the form of a phonograph record recording; nor may it be stored in a retrieval system, transmitted, or otherwise be copied for public or private use-other than for "fair use" as brief quotations embodied in articles and reviews-without prior written permission of the publisher, and or author.

The author of this book does not dispense medical advice or prescribe the use of any technique as a form of treatment for physical, emotional, or medical problems with the advice of a physician, either directly or indirectly. The intent of the author is only to offer information of a general nature to help you in your quest for emotional, physical, and spiritual well-being. In the event you use any of the information in this book for yourself, the author and publisher assume no responsibility for your actions.

Hardcover ISBN: 979-8-9901034-0-5
Paperback ISBN: 979-8-9901034-3-6
E-book ISBN: 979-8-9901034-2-9

1st edition, June 2024

Many, Many Thanks to:

My mother, the bravest person I know.

My wife, who believes in me more than I believe in myself.

My #1 Sweetie Pie, who when I'm down and out reminds me to drink my own Kool-Aid when she says "Daddy, you know you have to Pick Yourself."

David Denny, Sr., for directly demonstrating to me through his life what it is to truly be a coach, mentor, and friend.

My friends Edgar and Dannet, who had this vision for me before I had it for myself.

"We are all self-made, but only the successful will admit it." - Earl Nightingale

Rodney Goldston

CONTENTS

Nobody will Give You Permission xi
There's Greatness Inside You xiii
Now Is The Time xvii
How Great Are You? xxi
4 Elements Of Human Existence xxv

Section 1: The 7 SUCCESS Principles

Principle 1: Stupid People 3
Principle 2: Understand You Are A Brand In The Age of Google 31
Principle 3: Come Up With A Plan 43
Principle 4: Confront Challenges 61
Principle 5: Elevate Your Mind 81
Principle 6: Stop Living Your Fears 89
Principle 7: Sweat 99
The SUCCESS System Review 107

Section 2: Stepping Out Of Your Head

How You Got in Your Head? 113
The Domino Effect 117
The Power of Routine 125
Become an MVP 129
Get Your Beauty Rest 141

Section 3: Stepping Into Your Greatness

Follow The Light 147
Shine Your Light 155
Serving Your Way to Success 159
Be Uncommon 163
Uncommon People 167
Finding Beauty in Brokenness 207
Discovering, Crafting, and Sharing Your Story 213

Pick Yourself For Success

Time and Your Success 219
Thou Shall Steal.. 223
This Might Not Work... 229
Make a Decision 235
What's Your Azimuth? 241
Invest In Yourself 245
Outwork Everybody... 251
Beyond The Filtered Lens.. 255
Conclusion And Next Steps 259
PY4S Zone.. 263
About The Author 265
References... 267

Rodney Goldston

INTRODUCTION

NOBODY WILL GIVE YOU PERMISSION

Welcome to the "Pick Yourself For Success" system, a transformative journey crafted to guide you towards unleashing your true potential and realizing your aspirations. As you embark on this expedition, it's crucial to grasp that success isn't merely a destination, but a culmination of deliberate actions, mindset shifts, and strategic approaches. Your dreams won't materialize on their own; you must actively pursue them.

While success is often perceived as the ultimate achievement, within our system, it embodies more—it's a concept symbolized by an acronym, a roadmap comprised of seven pivotal elements fundamental to genuine success. Each letter signifies a vital piece of the puzzle leading you towards

Pick Yourself For Success

your greatness.

Success, in this context, transcends mere attainment of career milestones or financial prosperity; it encompasses a holistic transformation, blending personal growth, professional development, and a shift in mindset that propels you forward.

Remember the game "Mother May I" we played as children? The objective: reach "mother" (another player) by asking permission for your movements. You'd shout, "Mother, may I take three giant leaps forward?" only to hear, "No, but you can take three small steps backwards."

This seemingly simple game teaches a powerful lesson. We intuitively grasp the importance of bold action, the thrill of those giant leaps. Yet, the game also reinforces a hidden message: the act of asking permission. This ingrained habit can linger, silently shaping our behavior as adults. Many of us don't know how to pick ourselves for success because, deep down, we're still waiting for someone to grant us permission to leap.

To reach your desired destination—in your relationships, career, physical and spiritual well being, and finances—you must leap. However, no one will give you permission. You must choose yourself. Therefore, take that monumental leap today, for success awaits those courageous enough to embrace the journey of self-discovery and personal growth.

Rodney Goldston

START HERE

THERE'S GREATNESS INSIDE YOU

I told myself I was the greatest before I ever really was." - Muhammad Ali

I placed this section right up front before anything else in this book because if you don't read anything else, this is what I want you to know. More than just know, I want you to believe with your entire being that there's untapped greatness in you just waiting to be unleashed.

I believe within each person resides an untapped well of greatness, waiting to be unshackled and unfurled upon the world. But where does one begin to unleash this latent potential? The first and most pivotal step involves

Pick Yourself For Success

believing in this innate greatness. It's disheartening to encounter numerous individuals who fail to recognize their own significance, doubting their ability to make a meaningful impact in the world. Now let me be completely honest here, far too often this is me.

Muhammad Ali's quote resonates deeply because, in its brevity, it encapsulates a profound truth. He didn't proclaim greatness because he was already there; rather, he began by telling himself a different story. By embracing the notion that he was born great, Ali cultivated a mindset that propelled him to live up to that belief. He famously expressed disdain for the grueling hours of training, but within that toil, he found solace in the conviction that a few hours of dedicated practice could pave the way for a life lived as a champion. So, I implore you: What narrative are you scripting about yourself?

Ali's journey isn't just a testament to athletic prowess, but a testament to the power of self-belief. Ali recognized that to manifest greatness, he first had to proclaim it to himself.

Each person weaves their own story—a tale of triumphs, setbacks, hopes, and aspirations. Yet, embedded within these narratives are the underlying beliefs we hold about ourselves. These beliefs shape our reality, defining the limits of our potential and influencing the course of our lives. Are you telling yourself a story of limitation and self-doubt, or one that paints a vivid portrait of unyielding potential and boundless opportunity?

Rodney Goldston

Here's what my favorite book says in Proverbs 23:7. "As a man thinks in his heart, so is he." Now take a moment, say it out loud, and let those words sink into your heart and mind. God's words, not mine, tell you that whatever you think you are, you are.

Proverbs 23:7 is a general truth. That is to say it applies to everyone equally regardless of who you are, or your status in life. Each of us is the sum total of our thoughts.

It's this self-created narrative that directs our actions, defines our limitations, and ultimately molds our destinies.

As I write this, I'm so glad that many of my ancestors, slaves stolen from Africa, believed themselves to be more than the society around them believed them to be.

Now, say these words out loud with tremendous enthusiam. Yes, right now, out loud, using your big boy, or big girl voice. There's greatness inside me! I am beautiful! I am loved! I am blessed! And, as The Nortorious B.I.G put.."If you don't know, now you know."

Pick Yourself For Success

THE PICK YOURSELF FOR SUCCESS MINDSET

Now Is The Time

Waiting is the enemy of potential." - Rodney Goldston

Dr. Martin Luther King Jr.'s impactful words in "Why We Can't Wait" challenged societal norms, urging immediate action toward justice without waiting for approval. His narrative wasn't one of passivity but a call to seize the moment, to pick oneself and act.

The trailblazers of innovation and change consistently demonstrated this "Pick Yourself" mentality. They didn't wait for approval; they forged ahead, creating their paths in defiance of norms.

Their stories aren't mere triumphs, but blueprints for embracing the "Pick Yourself" mindset—from entrepreneurs who defied funding delays to activists who created movements. These individuals understood that waiting stifles potential.

THE FREEDOM 14

The Freedom 14, a group of determined students from Lincoln University in Pennsylvania, embarked on an extraordinary journey that exemplifies the transformative power of embracing the "Pick Yourself" mindset. Faced with a lack of funding for their university, these students refused to wait for a solution. Instead, they embarked on a grueling 66-mile walk from Chester County to the State Capitol in Harrisburg.

The backdrop to their trek was a bureaucratic impasse. A bill guaranteeing funding for several universities, including Lincoln, had stalled in the Pennsylvania General Assembly. The state House had passed the bill after schools froze tuition, but it languished in the Senate.

Undeterred, the Freedom 14 decided to take matters into their own hands. Their determined walk wasn't just a physical feat; it was a powerful statement advocating for their education and the future of Lincoln University. They arrived in Harrisburg on Sunday after starting their walk on Friday, highlighting their resilience and commitment.

What makes their story even more compelling is that Lincoln University was slated to receive the least amount of funding compared to other institutions – only $19 million compared to Penn State's $259 million. Yet, these students, who had the most to lose, demonstrated remarkable selflessness by fighting for all the underfunded schools.

Their bold action serves as a powerful reminder that even in the face of adversity, we have the power to create change when we "Pick Ourselves Up" and take action. The Freedom 14's journey embodies the core principles of self-reliance, resilience, and collective action—key tenets of the "Pick Yourself" philosophy. It's a testament to the transformative potential of embracing initiative and refusing to accept the status quo.

Embracing Self-Choice, Not Waiting for Validation

The crux of the matter is this: Are you waiting to be chosen or stepping up to choose yourself?

The journey to success often begins with a personal choice. It's about transcending conditioning, breaking free from the shackles of waiting, and boldly embracing the "Pick Yourself" mindset. It's understanding that greatness is often self-chosen, not externally validated.

Pick Yourself For Success

In this book, we'll explore steps toward self-empowerment, recognizing that the greatest achievements emerge from individuals who dare to choose themselves, take action, and carve their own paths, regardless of societal conditioning or the need for external validation.

GREATNESS GAUGE

HOW GREAT ARE YOU?

You've taken the first bold step toward transforming your life by picking up "Pick Yourself For Success." But before we embark on this journey together, I want to offer you something unique: a personalized roadmap to your greatness.

WELCOME TO THE GREATNESS GAUGE™ - YOUR PERSONAL COMPASS TO SUCCESS

The Greatness Gauge is more than just an assessment; it's a powerful tool designed to illuminate your unique strengths, uncover hidden potential, and pinpoint areas for growth. By blending cutting-edge neuroscience with timeless wisdom, this tool provides insights that are as unique as your

DNA.

WHY TAKE THE GREATNESS GAUGE BEFORE READING?

1. **Personalized Insights:** Just as a tailor measures before crafting the perfect suit, the Greatness Gauge measures your current mindset, strengths, and challenges. This allows you to tailor the strategies in this book to fit you perfectly.

2. **Focused Reading:** Know exactly which chapters will resonate most with your journey. Whether it's "Elevate Your Mind" or "Confront Challenges," you'll know where to focus for maximum impact.

3. **Benchmark Your Growth:** As you apply the SUCCESS system, retake the Gauge to see your progress. There's nothing more motivating than seeing your own growth!

4. **Community & Accountability:** Share your results (if you choose) to connect with others on similar paths. Remember, "S" isn't just for "Stupid People" - it's also for the "Support" you'll find in our community.

5. **Exclusive Resources:** Your results unlock personalized resources, worksheets, and even direct insights from me to supercharge your journey.

READY TO DISCOVER YOUR GREATNESS PROFILE?

1. Visit www.RodneyGoldston.com and click the link to the Greatness Gauge™.

2. Take the brief, insightful assessment.

3. Get your personalized Greatness Profile instantly.

Return to this book, armed with self-knowledge that will transform your reading experience.

Remember, you weren't born to be average. Inside you is a wellspring of potential, a unique greatness waiting to be unleashed. The Greatness Gauge is your first step in tapping into this potential.

So, before you turn the page, take a moment to understand yourself better. Because when you truly know yourself, picking yourself for success becomes not just a choice, but an inevitability.

YOUR GREATNESS AWAITS. LET'S UNLOCK IT TOGETHER.

Pick Yourself For Success

Rodney Goldston

THE CORE 4

4 Elements Of Human Existence

Before you embark on the journey through the SUCCESS system, it's crucial to uncover the foundational components that shape your existence—what I call your Core 4. This concept finds echoes in the Bible, where passages like 1 Thessalonians 5:23 speak of us as multifaceted beings with spirit, soul, and body. Envision your humanity as a symphony conducted by four distinct instruments: the Intellect, the Emotion, the Spirit, and the Physical. You recognize these as your mind, heart, soul, and body. Each plays a unique, yet interwoven, melody in the grand composition of your life.

What's intriguing is that these elements aren't solitary players; they're interconnected, harmonizing together to create the beautiful symphony of your existence. But here's the catch: it's entirely possible to excel in one aspect and yet falter in another.

Take, for instance, a preacher delivering profound sermons, guiding their congregations with tremendous spiritual wisdom—a master of the spiritual. Yet, despite their spiritual prowess, they struggle with their physical fitness. This imbalance, this lack of harmony between the spirit and the body, is glaring. After all, the Bible reminds us in 1 Corinthians 6:19 that our bodies are "temples of the Holy Spirit" (ESV).

Conversely, you may have encountered individuals fervently focused on physical fitness and immaculate diets—epitomes of physical perfection. However, their spirit seems to yearn for nurturing, and their emotions crave depth. It's the imbalance between these cores that disrupts the symphony.

Consider also the high-powered executive, a titan of industry who commands respect in the boardroom. Their intellect is undeniable, their strategic mind a marvel. Yet, their relentless pursuit of success may leave their personal lives neglected. Relationships suffer, emotional connections weaken. This imbalance between the intellectual and emotional aspects throws the symphony off-key.

We might also see this in the passionate artist, their soul ablaze with creative fire. Their emotions flow freely onto the canvas, their hearts pour into every note. However, a dedication solely to the emotional expression might leave their technical skills underdeveloped. The intellectual growth needed to refine their craft is neglected. This imbalance between the emotional and intellectual aspects can leave their artistic expression unfulfilled.

As you delve into the SUCCESS system, let's explore the Intellect, the Emotion, the Spirit, and the Physical, not as disparate entities seeking equilibrium, but as partners in a harmonious dance. Let's embrace the melodies of life, understanding that success isn't found in the perfect balance but in the harmonious resonance of your Core 4. Furthermore, as you navigate each chapter or element within the SUCCESS system, I'll accompany you at the end of every chapter on the seven success principles, clarifying how that specific element relates to your Core 4. This integration will shed light on how each principle intertwines with these fundamental aspects of your being, fostering a deeper understanding of how to achieve harmony and growth across all dimensions of your life.

Pick Yourself For Success

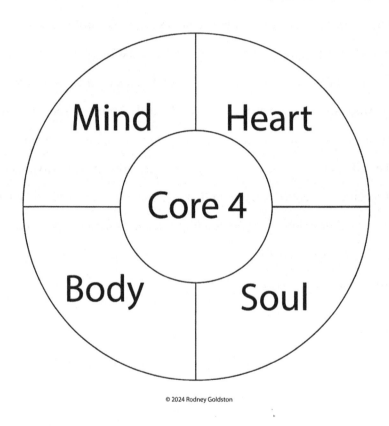

SECTION ONE

7 SUCCESS PRINCIPLES

CHAPTER 1

PRINCIPLE 1: STUPID PEOPLE

"Never argue with stupid people, they will drag you down to their level and beat you with experience." - Mark Twain

My wife detests when I label people as stupid. But let's be blunt—some individuals are just, well, stupid. Mark Twain, with his sharp wit, once cautioned, "Never argue with stupid people, they will drag you down to their level and beat you with experience." It's a statement that resonates with the truth of countless unproductive discussions you may have encountered, both personally and professionally.

Pick Yourself For Success

This chapter acts as a manifesto for the art of restraint, guiding you to identify futile battlegrounds and opt not to engage in them. It's about recognizing that every moment spent in a pointless argument detracts from your pursuit of greatness. It's about urging you to focus on growth rather than futile debates.

At its essence, Twain's words serve as a cautionary signal, prompting you to weigh the cost of engaging in futile debates. The 'stupid people' he refers to aren't necessarily lacking intelligence; rather, they are unwilling or unable to engage in reasoned discourse. Reflecting on this quote encourages you to differentiate between meaningful discussions that propel you forward and fruitless arguments that only anchor you to the mundane.

Consider this: every moment spent arguing with someone incapable of understanding your perspective detracts from your journey of personal growth. These unproductive debates act as barriers, impeding progress and diverting valuable energy toward a battle you cannot win. Understanding this dynamic is crucial, as it positions personal growth and success as casualties in the verbal skirmish with those unwilling to comprehend.

Choosing Battles Wisely

Navigating life's battles requires discernment. Twain's wisdom emphasizes the significance of choosing where to direct your mental and emotional energy wisely. By bypassing trivial disputes, you preserve the vital resources necessary for pursuits that genuinely contribute to your aspirations.

This discussion aims to provide you with a guiding compass for traversing the intricate landscape of discourse. It's not merely about evading arguments to maintain harmony; it's a conscious decision to avoid conflicts that jeopardize your journey toward personal growth and success.

Identifying Unproductive Discourse

In the intricate dance of discourse, mastering the art of recognizing unproductive and futile conversations is paramount. Let's delve into the process of identifying 'stupid' arguments, understanding their telltale signs, and distinguishing them from the fertile grounds of constructive dialogue.

Unproductive conversations often manifest through unmistakable signs. Keep an eye out for circular arguments that never seem to find resolution, a resistance to alternative viewpoints, and a lack of constructive contributions. These are the warning signs indicating you might be stepping into a swamp of fruitless discussion.

'Stupid' arguments aren't characterized by a lack of intelligence but rather by a dearth of open-mindedness and rationality. They thrive on repetition, dismiss factual evidence, and revel in perpetuating confusion. Recognizing these traits can serve as a compass, guiding you away from the abyss of unproductive dialogue.

In contrast, constructive dialogue is distinguished by a genuine exchange of ideas, a willingness to entertain alternative viewpoints, and a mutual commitment to seeking common ground or solutions. Engaging in fruitful conversation yields a sense of progress, a forward momentum absent in the stagnant waters of unproductivity.

THE ENERGY DRAIN OF STUPIDITY

Likely the most insidious consequence of fruitless arguments is that they drain you of your precious energy. You pay an emotional toll every time you engage in an argument with those who resist reason, and there's a negative impact on your mental health and well-being. Successful people have learned to preserve their energy by not engaging in useless circular arguments.

Engaging in arguments with individuals resistant to reason can be emotionally taxing. The frustration stemming from the inability to communicate effectively, coupled with the futility of attempting to impart logic, can create a disheartening cocktail of emotions. This emotional drain not only affects the immediate conversation but lingers, casting a shadow over subsequent interactions.

Prolonged exposure to unproductive discussions takes a toll on mental health also. It can contribute to heightened stress levels, increased anxiety, and a sense of helplessness. The persistent clash with irrationality can create a toxic environment within the mind, hindering clarity of thought and impeding your ability to focus on meaningful pursuits.

Tuning into the Right Frequency

Nikola Tesla is quoted as saying, "If you want to find the secrets of the universe, think in terms of energy, frequency, and vibration." While this quote might initially seem abstract, the concept of vibration is fundamental to our understanding of the universe. We experience vibrations in everyday life through sound waves and light. Furthermore, humans are highly sensitive to emotional cues, picking up on subtle vibrations in communication. Our experiences and interactions undoubtedly influence our emotional state, much like tuning a dial, but the exact relationship between emotions and frequencies is a complex topic that scientists are still exploring. The individuals I'm referring to as "stupid" in this chapter aren't necessarily lacking intelligence in the traditional sense. Rather, they're vibrating on frequencies that clash with the trajectory you desire for your journey toward success. Their negativity, cynicism, or defeatist attitudes send out signals that disrupt our own vibrational alignment.

One of my preferred methods for resonating positively is during my morning walks; I simply ask Siri to play positive vibrations. You, too, can easily access positive frequencies through your favorite streaming services or platforms like YouTube, deliberately selecting sounds that vibrate within a range conducive to positivity and success.

You might initially be skeptical about this talk of frequencies. Yet, think about how you tune in to your favorite radio station. You adjust the dial until you're receiving the desired signal. Essentially, you're choosing which wavelength or "station" to tune into. This concept is akin to adjusting your vibrational frequency.

It's said that Albert Einstein once remarked, "Everything in life is vibration." Even one of the greatest minds in history recognized the profound impact of vibrational frequencies in shaping our world.

If you're striving for success, if you're aiming to manifest greatness, it's crucial to be mindful of the frequencies you tune into. Just as you'd switch the radio station to match your preferred music genre, consider altering your vibrational frequency. Surround yourself with individuals and energies that resonate with your goals, propelling you toward the wavelength of success.

Connection to Success

The connection between energy preservation and success is profound. Success often demands sustained focus, resilience in the face of challenges, and a steadfast commitment to long-term goals. Engaging in arguments that sap our energy jeopardizes our capacity to meet these demands. By recognizing the emotional and mental toll of fruitless debates, you empower yourself to redirect your energy toward endeavors that propel you forward on the path to success.

In the pursuit of your goals, every ounce of energy is a valuable currency. Preserving this currency becomes a strategic move, ensuring that it is invested where it can yield the greatest returns. As you navigate away from the energy drain of unproductive discussions, you pave the way for a more focused, resilient, and successful journey.

Energy Preservation and Return On Energy

Just as a battery must be wisely conserved for when it's truly needed, so too must your mental and emotional energy. Preserving energy becomes a critical practice, recognizing that every argument, no matter how well-intentioned, is not worth the expenditure of this finite resource. This concept serves as a lifeline, reminding you to be a mindful custodian of your mental and emotional well-being.

The idea of Return on Energy (ROE) was first explained to me many years ago during a job interview. The concept emphasizes that in the pursuit of success, not only must we be vigilant guardians of our energy, but we must also become astute investors, considering the concept of ROE. While Return On Investment (ROI) is a well-understood business principle, ROE often takes a backseat, overlooked in the hustle and bustle of daily interactions. It's an important concept, so I want to take some time here to unpack it, ensuring you have a firm grasp on what it is and why it's crucial in your journey toward success.

THE OVERLOOKED ROE

In the business world, ROI is a familiar metric, assessing the profitability of an investment. In the realm of personal growth and success, the parallel concept of ROE measures the return you receive on the energy you invest in conversations, relationships, and pursuits. It's the overlooked currency that can make or break your journey.

Just as in business, where wise investments yield favorable returns, certain conversations and engagements have a ROE that surpasses the energy invested. These are the interactions that leave you inspired, motivated, and energized. They contribute to your growth, deepen our understanding, and propel us forward. Recognizing and prioritizing these positive ROE engagements is an essential aspect of strategic living.

STRATEGIC SURROUNDINGS FOR POSITIVE ROE

Strategically surrounding yourself with individuals who offer a positive ROE becomes a key aspect of curating your social and professional circles. Much like a skilled investor diversifies their portfolio for maximum returns, you must diversify your relationships to ensure a net positive return on your energy investments. This doesn't imply avoiding challenging conversations but rather being discerning about where you allocate your precious energy.

NAVIGATING THE UNPRODUCTIVE

Next, let's delve into mastering the art of strategic avoidance by exploring some practical tips to disengage from fruitless discussions. I'll also guide you towards alternative approaches for redirecting your energy and emphasize the vital importance of surrounding yourself with positive influences. This includes fostering drama-free environments and nurturing relationships that uplift and support your growth.

Practical Tips for Disengagement

1. Choose Your Battles Wisely: Not every disagreement deserves a battlefield. Gauge the significance of the issue and assess whether it's worth investing your energy in a potentially unproductive conversation.

2. Recognize Warning Signs: Develop a keen sense for recognizing signs of unproductive dialogue early on. Circular arguments, a lack of receptivity, and a refusal to acknowledge facts are indicators that it might be time to disengage.

3. Master the Art of Polite Exit: Learn to gracefully exit conversations that show signs of turning unproductive. A simple "I appreciate your perspective, but I need to focus on [insert priority]" can be a polite way to disengage without escalating tensions.

Approaches for Redirecting Energy

Channel Energy into Productive Pursuits

When faced with the prospect of an unproductive discussion, consciously redirect your energy toward more constructive endeavors. Whether it's a work project, a personal goal, or a creative pursuit, use that energy to fuel endeavors that bring tangible results.

Practice Mindful Breathing

In moments of frustration, employ mindfulness techniques like deep breathing. This not only helps diffuse immediate tension but also provides a moment for reflection before deciding whether or not to engage.

Cultivate a 'Pause and Reflect' Habit

Before jumping into potentially draining conversations, make it a habit to pause and reflect. As Ben Franklin wisely noted, "When angry, count to ten before you speak; when very angry, one hundred." Stephen Covey echoed this sentiment in his book The 7 Habits of Highly Effective People, stating, "Between stimulus and response, there is a space. In that space is our power to choose our response. In our response lies our growth and our freedom."

Drama-Free Environments and Relationships

Seek Drama-Free People

Be intentional about the company you keep, actively seeking out drama-free individuals. Among our close friends, a small group of just two other couples, raising our glasses and saying "cheers" signifies more than just the end of a conversation. It's a shared commitment to fostering a positive and drama-free atmosphere within our circle.

Seek Drama-Free Environments

Tranquility is a deliberate choice. I'm blessed that I can choose to live in environments that offer peace and easy access to nature. But everyone can't. If you're someone who can't consider leaving your hectic environment to head to a park, museum (my personal favorite), or any place that will allow you to temporarily disengage from the drama of your environment.

Seek Mentors and Positive Role Models

Align yourself with mentors and role models who not only inspire, but also cultivate a drama-free atmosphere. Their influence can serve as a guiding light, nurturing a serene environment conducive to both personal and professional growth. Oprah Winfrey famously advises, "Surround yourself only with successful people," highlighting the importance of the company you keep. Similarly, motivational speaker Les Brown emphasizes that you'll become the average of the five people you spend the most time with. In other words, ensure that the individuals in your inner circle are those from whom you can learn and grow.

In mastering the art of strategic avoidance and fostering drama-free environments, you not only conserve your precious energy but also establish a fertile ground where success can thrive. By channeling your focus into constructive pursuits and surrounding yourself with positive influences, you cultivate an atmosphere primed for growth, achievement, and overall wellness. Here's to nurturing a tribe that uplifts, inspires, and drives you onward in your journey! Cheers to your continued success!

Learning from Experience: The Wisdom of Job

In the Book of Job in the Old Testament, we encounter a profound narrative that unfolds with Job, a righteous man, facing a series of devastating trials. Job's friends, attempting to make sense of his suffering, engage in debates with him about the reasons behind his hardships.

Job's friends, although well-intentioned, represent a form of uninformed perspectives. They argue from a limited understanding, insisting that Job's suffering must be a result of his own wrongdoing. Despite Job's protests and efforts to explain his innocence, they remain wrong, and steadfast in their convictions.

My friend Don taught me that when pondering scripture, it's crucial to ask: 'What's the purpose of this story? What is it trying to teach me?' Here are several valuable lessons we can derive from the story of Job.

1. Job's story emphasizes the limits of human wisdom. Despite his friends' attempts to provide explanations, their understanding is incomplete. The narrative highlights the futility of arguing with the uninformed when perspectives are grounded in partial knowledge (remember my definition of stupid people?).

2. Job's steadfastness in the face of adversity showcases the importance of endurance and faith. Rather than engaging in futile debates, Job focuses on maintaining his trust in God, demonstrating that personal growth often arises from enduring challenges with resilience and faith.

3. As the story unfolds, God speaks directly to Job, revealing the complexity of His divine plan. Job's suffering was not a direct result of his actions but part of a larger cosmic design beyond human comprehension. The lesson here is that sometimes, accepting the mystery of God's plan is wiser than engaging in fruitless debates.

4. Job's response to God's revelation is marked by humility. He acknowledges the limitations of human understanding and repents of any presumptuous thoughts. The narrative suggests that true wisdom lies in recognizing our finite knowledge and humbly submitting to the divine.

In reflecting on Job's story, we find an excellent illustration of the futility of arguing with the uninformed and the profound lessons that can be extracted from such experiences. The narrative encourages us to approach life's challenges with endurance, faith, and humility, recognizing that the fullness of understanding often lies beyond our human grasp.

So we've covered what you should tune out, now let's turn our attention to what you should tune into.

The Power of Selective Listening: Tuning Into Success

There are a lot of voices that surround you daily, the skill of selective listening emerges as a powerful tool for maintaining focus on your personal goals. Selective listening isn't merely about hearing; it's about consciously filtering out the noise that hinders your journey and staying true to the path of success.

Selective listening involves intentionally directing your attention toward what aligns with your goals and aspirations while purposefully filtering out distractions and unproductive chatter. It's not about closing yourself off to diverse perspectives but rather about safeguarding your mental space and energy for endeavors that propel you forward.

Here's some advice for filtering out the noise.

First, selective listening begins with a clear understanding of your priorities. By identifying your personal and professional goals, you gain clarity on the messages that deserve your attention.

Second, channel your energy toward sources of positivity and inspiration. Whether it's engaging with uplifting content, surrounding yourself with encouraging individuals, or seeking out motivational resources, focus on what fuels your motivation.

Third, recognize conversations or influences that drain your energy without contributing to your growth. Selective listening involves discerning when to disengage from unproductive discussions and redirecting your focus toward constructive endeavors.

STRATEGIC SILENCE

In the art of selective listening, strategic silence plays a crucial role. Knowing when not to engage with information or individuals that don't contribute positively to your journey is a skill that can shield you from unnecessary distractions.

Consider the wisdom of Warren Buffett, who once remarked, "The difference between successful people and really successful people is that really successful people say no to almost everything." This sentiment encapsulates the essence of selective listening—saying no to the noise and yes to the pursuits that truly matter.

Personally, I have chosen to selectively listen almost exclusively to Seth Godin in matters of marketing, Warren Buffett in matters of investing, and

Dr. King in matters of society. This intentional focus has allowed me to gain deep insights from these authorities in their respective fields.

Embarking on a Journey of Selective Reading

Imagine the impact of not just selectively listening but also selectively reading. What if, instead of consuming a variety of perspectives from multiple authors, you chose to delve deeply into the works of a single, influential figure? Consider the wealth of knowledge that could be gleaned by immersing yourself entirely in the writings of Dr. Martin Luther King or Nelson Mandela. This level of selective focus in reading is a path that promises not only depth of understanding but also a profound resonance with the wisdom of a singular guiding voice.

In weaving the power of selective listening and reading into your daily life, you fortify your ability to stay true to your path. By consciously choosing what you absorb and filtering out the distractions, you carve a focused and purposeful trajectory toward success. It's not about closing yourself off; it's about opening yourself up to the right influences and insights that propel you forward on our journey.

LEADERS LISTEN TO UNDERSTAND

In the pursuit of success and personal growth, effective communication stands as a cornerstone. However, communication isn't merely about speaking; it's equally—if not more—about listening. This crucial aspect often receives insufficient attention in our education and training, leaving many without the necessary skills to truly understand others. Think about it. You've taken courses on how to write, read, and speak, but if you're like most folks you've never taken a course on how to listen.

Sam Harrison in his book Idea Spotting: How To Find Your Next Great Idea explains that we normally listen at one of four levels.

1. We ignore the person

2. We pretend to listen

3. We selectively listen

4. We attentively listen

Experts like Stephen Covey suggested a fifth more effective level of listening called empathetic listening. Let's jump into some of the ideas around empathetic listening as Covey explained them.

Seek First To Understand, Then Be Understood

Shortly after I graduated from college and got started in a career in sales, someone gave me a copy of a book called The 7 Habits of Highly Successful People. I think the book sat on my bookshelf for two years before I got around to reading it. But man, when I did, I found the principles in the book life-changing.

Habit number 5, Seek First To Understand, Then Be Understood shines a light on the vital role of attentive listening in effective leadership. Rather than focusing solely on getting their own point across, true leaders prioritize understanding others' perspectives first.

A common pitfall in communication is the tendency to listen with the intent to reply rather than to understand. This approach often leads to selective hearing, where individuals filter information through their own life experiences and biases, hindering genuine understanding (they become the 'stupid people').

Autobiographical responses, while sometimes appropriate, can pose a barrier to empathetic listening. When individuals relate everything they hear back to their own experiences, they may miss the deeper meaning behind the speaker's words.

In the journey to escape the difficulty of fruitless interactions and navigate challenging conversations effectively, adopting the mindset of a leader who listens can be transformative. By prioritizing understanding over being understood, leaders cultivate empathy, build trust, and foster meaningful connections with others.

APPLYING THE CONCH PRINCIPLE IN EVERYDAY LIFE

Reflecting on my high school reading experiences, I recalled a powerful symbol from the novel "Lord of the Flies"—the conch. In the story, this shell serves as a tool for facilitating communication among a group of boys stranded on an uninhabited island.

Inspired by the conch's significance, I devised a practical application of this symbol in my own life, particularly during heated debates with my wife. Implementing a makeshift conch rule, we employed any nearby object—a book, a deck of cards, a pencil—to represent the conch.

The rules were simple: the person holding the conch had the floor to express their thoughts while the other listened intently. To ensure mutual understanding, the listener would then summarize the speaker's points before transitioning to their own perspective. If the summary fell short, the conch remained with the speaker until clarity was achieved. This process continued until both parties felt understood and respected.

By incorporating the conch principle into our discussions, my wife and I not only fostered attentive listening but also nurtured empathy and cooperation. This simple yet effective technique transformed our conflicts into opportunities for mutual understanding and growth, reinforcing the importance of Habit 5 in everyday interactions.

Epictetus' Wisdom: Listening Twice as Much as We Speak

Epictetus, the ancient Stoic philosopher, once said, "We have two ears and one mouth so that we can listen twice as much as we speak." This profound insight underscores the essence of Covey's Habit 5 and the principles discussed here.

In a world often dominated by the clamor of one's own voice, Epictetus reminds us of the importance of humility and receptivity. By listening more than you speak, you open yourself to the wisdom and perspectives of others, enriching your understanding and fostering deeper connections.

This wisdom aligns perfectly with Covey's Habit 5, emphasizing the primacy of understanding before seeking to be understood. By embracing this principle and embodying the spirit of attentive listening, you not only enhance your communication skills but also nurture relationships built on empathy, respect, and mutual growth.

Drawing from the principles outlined in Habit 5 and the article "Habit 5: Seek First to Understand, Then to Be Understood" from the Franklin Covey website, here are ten tips for listening like a leader:

1. Practice Active Listening: Give your full attention to the speaker and demonstrate genuine interest in understanding their perspective.

2. Suspend Judgment: Avoid forming premature judgments or assumptions while listening, allowing the speaker to fully express themselves.

3. Focus on Understanding: Shift your focus from seeking to be understood to seeking first to understand the other person's thoughts and feelings.

4. Empathize with the Speaker: Put yourself in the speaker's shoes and strive to see the situation from their perspective.

5. Ask Clarifying Questions: Seek clarification by asking open-ended questions that encourage the speaker to elaborate on their thoughts and feelings.

6. Validate Feelings: Acknowledge the speaker's emotions and validate their feelings, even if you may not agree with their perspective.

7. Avoid Interrupting: Resist the urge to interrupt or interject your own opinions while the speaker is talking, allowing them to express themselves fully.

8. Reflective Listening: Paraphrase the speaker's words to ensure accurate understanding and demonstrate active engagement.

9. Seek Common Ground: Look for areas of agreement and shared understanding, fostering mutual respect and rapport.

10. Follow Up: Summarize your understanding of the speaker's message and express appreciation for their perspective, reinforcing the connection.

Additionally, Kate Murphy offers an insightful perspective in her book You're Not Listening that in modern life we're always encouraged to listen to our heart, our guts, the little voice within us, but we're rarely encouraged to listen to other people. This further underscores the profound impact of listening in your daily life.

Kate's writings also help to teach that listening isn't just a passive activity but a dynamic process that shapes your interactions, relationships, and ultimately, your life's trajectory. As she puts it, how well you listen, to whom, and in what circumstances can profoundly influence your experiences and outcomes, for better or worse.

When considering Mark Twain's caution against arguing with stupid people, Murphy's perspective adds another layer of depth. Engaging in futile arguments with individuals who are unwilling or unable to engage in reasoned discourse not only drains your energy but also reflects a failure to listen effectively. By allowing yourself to be drawn into unproductive debates, you forfeit the opportunity to truly understand others and, in turn, to navigate your interactions in a more constructive manner.

The essence of what I'm trying to convey to you is the importance of discernment in choosing when and with whom to engage in conversation. Just as Twain warns against futile arguments, Murphy reminds us that the quality of our listening, particularly in challenging situations, can significantly impact the course of our lives. By honing your listening skills and exercising discernment in your interactions, you empower yourself to navigate life's complexities more effectively and to avoid being "dragged down" by unproductive engagements.

In essence, both Twain's admonition and Murphy's observation underscore the power of listening—to yourself, to others, and to the circumstances in which you find yourself. By heeding their insights, you can strive to become more adept at discerning when to engage, when to disengage, and when to listen with empathy and understanding, thereby charting a course toward greater fulfillment and success.

Power Tip

Practice empathetic listening with two people today.

Don't Take My Word For It...Take God's

We've already examined the wisdom in the book of Job regarding stupid people, but you might be surprised to learn that the Bible offers more timeless wisdom that aligns perfectly with the theme of Chapter 1— **"S - Stop Listening to Stupid People."**

Discernment and Wise Counsel

The book of Proverbs serves as a treasury of wisdom, guiding us to discern the difference between foolishness and wisdom. Proverbs 12:15 urges us to recognize that the way of fools may seem right to them, but the truly wise are those who listen to advice. As you embark on your journey of self-improvement, consider the profound impact of seeking and heeding wise counsel.

Guarding Your Heart and Mind

Proverbs 4:23 cautions us to "guard our hearts, for everything flows from it." In the context of escaping the quagmire of fruitless discussions, this principle becomes paramount. By safeguarding your heart and mind, you fortify yourself against the allure of unwise counsel that could lead you astray from your path to success.

Choosing Companions Wisely

The people you surround yourself with profoundly shape your journey. As Proverbs 13:20 wisely advises, "Walk with the wise and become wise, for a companion of fools suffers harm." That's basically saying walk alongside the people who are already successful at the thing you want to do.

Incorporating these timeless biblical principles into Chapter 1 adds depth and wisdom to your narrative. Reflecting on themes of discernment, seeking wise counsel, and considering the influence of your companions, I hope these insights inspire and guide you as you navigate away from unproductive interactions.

Lastly I'd like to leave you with this thought provoking nugget to chew on. Sidney Poitier beautifully captured this very dynamic in his book "The Measure Of A Man." He wrote, "If you walk down the street and someone is with you, he'll adjust to your pace or you to his and you'll never be aware of it. There's no effort, it simply happens. And, the same thing can happen with the rhythm of your life."

Power Tip

Take a moment to consider: Who are you walking with? Whose pace have you adjusted to?

Harmonizing Your Core 4

In this chapter, we explored the intricacies of managing challenging interactions, emphasizing the importance of selective listening and discerning engagements that truly align with your goals. This aligns with the Heart or Emotional core of the Core 4, emphasizing emotional control, empathy, and understanding in handling difficult situations.

Cultivating emotional intelligence is crucial. To enhance your Emotional core, practice active listening in your interactions. Take a moment before responding, empathize with others' perspectives, and remain mindful of your emotional reactions.

Be intentional about what you absorb and engage with. This involves not only filtering external conversations but also being mindful of your internal dialogue. Focus on positive affirmations and nurturing self-talk to foster emotional balance.

Pick Yourself For Success

Remember, growth in this aspect isn't about avoiding difficult interactions but rather about developing the emotional resilience to navigate them effectively. Seek opportunities that challenge your emotional intelligence, allowing for continual growth.

By harmonizing your Heart or Emotional core, you're not just cultivating emotional control but also refining your interactions, ensuring that they align with your personal and professional aspirations. This balanced integration among the Core 4 aspects drives holistic growth, aligning your personal development journey with the principles of the SUCCESS system.

Don't forget to visit my website at, www.rodneygoldston.com, and complete the Greatness Gauge™.

CHAPTER 2

Principle 2: Understand You Are A Brand In The Age of Google

"Google never forgets." - Seth Godin

In the ever-shifting landscape of the digital era, understanding the importance of personal branding isn't just a savvy choice; it's become a necessity.

Imagine the internet as a vast quilt, intricately stitching together aspects of your life through search engines, social media platforms, and online communities. The information people uncover about you isn't arbitrary; it profoundly influences their perception of you, the opportunities you're presented with, and whether you receive support or encounter obstacles.

Take a moment to Google your name and examine what surfaces. If the results don't align with how you want to be perceived, it's time to take action, my friend. Keep in mind that the initial step for someone considering hiring you, engaging in business with you, or entering into a relationship with you is likely to involve Googling your name or searching for you on social media platforms.

VISIBILITY AND REPUTATION

Google isn't just a search engine; it's the lens through which the world catches a glimpse of you. Whether through personal websites, social media, or the various online platforms you engage with, it's about understanding the subtle art of digital presence without turning it into a constant self-promotion.

Building a personal brand isn't about putting on a mask; it's about strategically showcasing the most authentic version of yourself. It's an ongoing commitment where consistent efforts align your digital activities with personal and professional goals, not just to sell but to share and connect genuinely.

Establishing Trust and Credibility

Whether you're aware of it or not, you embody a personal brand. The degree to which others trust you, your brand equity, determines their willingness to engage with you. This fundamental principle is often the cornerstone of sales training: "People do business with people they like and trust." This adage seamlessly extends to realms beyond sales, such as hiring decisions and admissions processes.

So, how does one cultivate trust and likability in today's digital landscape? The answer lies in the realm of the Internet. In this era, trust and credibility are not just abstract concepts; they are the currency of meaningful interactions.

Trust flourishes when authenticity, consistency, and a genuine concern for value addition are evident. However, it's crucial to remember that you're more than just a brand; you're a living, dynamic individual with autonomy, the capacity for growth, and the potential to effect change. Reducing yourself to a mere brand, focused solely on profit or image-building, limits your true potential.

Smile You're On Candid Camera

Way back in the day when I was a kid the prank show Candid Camera was a hit. Everybody watched it. If you've never seen it head over to Youtube and watch an episode or two. The catchphrase was "Smile, You're On Candid Camera." Back then, it was a reminder that you might be caught in a funny or awkward moment for a TV show. Today, it's not just a phrase; it's quite literally a way of life.

In this era where everyone walks around with a camera in their pocket connected to the internet, it's imperative to conduct yourself like you're on Candid Camera—because, in essence, you actually are. The potential of being recorded, photographed, or captured in some digital form is ever-present. Your actions, words, and decisions can become a permanent part of the digital landscape.

Lessons from Amy Cooper

Amy Cooper, is a woman whose story became a symbol of the impact of what happens when we forget that our offline actions are easily captured and posted to the Internet.

Rodney Goldston

In a Central Park encounter, Amy, a white woman, encountered Christian Cooper, a Black man, who politely asked her to leash her dog, as per park rules.

The situation escalated, and Amy, pretending to feel threatened, called the police. However, what unfolded during this encounter was captured on video by Christian. Amy's behavior, fueled by fear and bias, went viral. The repercussions of her actions were swift and severe—she faced public condemnation, lost her job, and became synonymous with the dangers of weaponizing privilege.

Amy's Google search unearthed more than just her professional background—it laid bare a moment of flawed judgment exposed for the world to witness. Now, I can't claim to know Amy personally, and I'm not here to pass judgment on her character. However, her story serves as a sobering illustration of the point I'm striving to convey: in the age of Google, our online actions have the potential to create enduring impressions. It's a sobering reminder to approach the digital realm with mindfulness and careful consideration.

Whether in personal or professional settings, the choices you make online and off contribute to the narrative you're crafting. Amy's lapse in judgment, amplified by the digital lens, serves as a powerful lesson about the potential repercussions of our actions in the interconnected web of the internet.

As you embrace the concept of "U - Understand You're a Brand in the Age of Google," recognize that your digital presence is a canvas. It's not just a space for data; it's where you artistically paint the portrait of your personal brand. It's imperative that you grasp the significance of personal branding in this digital era and draw insights from the cautionary tale of Amy Cooper and position yourself not merely as a passive consumer but as the curator of your own narrative—a brand with the prowess to mold perceptions, open doors, and etch your journey to success in the age of Google.

CASE STUDIES OF THOSE WHO HAVE SUCCESSFULLY LEVERAGED THEIR PERSONAL BRANDS

When it comes to understanding personal branding, real-life examples can be the most enlightening. Let's take a look at a variety of people who have effectively used intentional personal branding to make an impact, coming from different backgrounds and fields.

OPRAH WINFREY: THE QUEEN OF AUTHENTICITY

Although Oprah didn't primarily build her brand on the Internet, she is the go-to when it comes to understanding what it means to literally grow a personal brand from nothing to a billion dollar personal brand. In fact Oprah's personal brand is so strong you don't even have to say her full name, nor her first name to know who she is, someone need only say the letter 'O' and we know just who they are referring to.

What I love about Oprah is that she stands as an iconic figure whose personal brand radiates authenticity and genuine connection. Her journey from a local news anchor to the global powerhouse she is today is a testament to the potency of a well-crafted personal brand. Oprah's authenticity, vulnerability, and unwavering commitment to uplifting others have solidified her as a beacon of inspiration. Her digital presence, spanning social media, a personal website, and various philanthropic endeavors, showcases the power of aligning your brand with your core values.

Aaron Marino: Crafting an Alpha Identity

I started following Aaron when he was making videos in what looked like his living room. I've watched hundreds of his videos about shoes, belts, shirts, suits, you name it.

Aaron, is the force behind Alpha M. In every conceivable way he exemplifies the fusion of personal passion and brand identity. As a style and image consultant, Aaron's journey is a compelling case study in how personal branding can transcend industries. Through his YouTube channel, website, and engaging social media content, Aaron has curated a distinct online persona that resonates with his audience. By authentically sharing his expertise and experiences, he has not only built a successful brand but has become a trusted authority in the realm of men's style and self-improvement.

Issa Rae: Redefining Narratives

Issa Rae, the creator and star of the critically acclaimed series "Insecure," has leveraged her personal brand to redefine narratives and amplify underrepresented voices. Through her online presence, including social media and a robust digital platform, Issa has become a trailblazer in the entertainment industry. Her journey illustrates how personal branding can be a catalyst for breaking barriers and reshaping industries. What I love about what she's accomplished is that she proves that you can turn the camera on and just be you.

Gary Vaynerchuk: From Wine Library to Digital Mogul

When I was trying to figure out this Internet thing I watched Gary's videos relentlessly. But who hasn't. And that's the point Gary's brand is so ubiquitous now that you forget there was a time when he was just some kid selling wine for his parents with a wild idea of maybe doing some explainer videos that would increase wine sales. Gary's journey underscores the transformative power of consistent and intentional personal branding.

Justin Bieber: A YouTube Discovery

This one here is for my daughter who, when she was young, was a huge Justin Bieber fan. Justin Bieber's ascent to stardom is synonymous with the transformative impact of personal branding in the digital age.

What you likely don't know is that his mother was posting videos of him on YouTube and some guy named Usher (yea, that Usher) saw a video and well you and the entire world know the rest of the story.

Seth Godin: Daily Blogging Maven

I read his blog every day. I buy every book he writes. Seth is a marketing maven. He's the guy all of us marketers listen to. He has cultivated his personal brand through the power of daily blogging. His commitment to consistently sharing insights, thoughts, and reflections has not only established him as a thought leader in marketing but also emphasizes the cumulative impact of persistent digital engagement.

Myron Golden: The Art of Persuasion

One of my favorites to follow, Myron Golden, a master of persuasive communication, adds his distinctive touch to our array of case studies. Through his expertise in sales and communication, Myron has crafted a personal brand that goes beyond industry boundaries. His journey exemplifies the transformative potential of intentional personal branding in the pursuit of professional success.

Tabitha Brown's Influence Beyond the Kitchen

Tabitha Brown's impact extends far beyond her delicious vegan recipes. Her signature food seasoning, Sunshine, has become a staple in many kitchens, including mine, adding flavor and warmth to countless dishes. Moreover, Tabitha's collaborations with Target have further elevated her brand, offering a range of products, from animal-friendly clothing to kitchenware, that align with her values of compassion and sustainability. What's remarkable is that Tabitha began her journey on social media, simply being herself—a testament to the authentic power of personal branding and the potential for genuine connection to resonate and thrive in the digital age.

These case studies underscore the universality of personal branding principles, regardless of race, sex, or industry. Each narrative reinforces the notion that intentional and authentic digital presence can transcend boundaries, opening doors to unprecedented opportunities in the age of Google.

Does God Care About Your Personal Brand?

Did you know that Jacob, one of the fathers of the Israel nation, had a name that was once synonymous with trickery and deceit? Yes, Jacob was so horrible that when someone did something low down, or dirty folks would be like "Man, you did a Jacob!"

Jacob's personal brand was so bad that God had to actually change his name. In a strange event that happens overnight, Jacob wrestles with a mysterious figure. When morning comes, he gets a new name — Israel. This change isn't just about a different name; it shows a big change in who he has become. From being a trickster (Jacob) to someone who struggles with God (Israel), this old story captures how people can change, how important identity is, and that God cares about our personal brands.

The Timeless Relevance of Personal Branding

Though the term "personal branding" may seem like a recent addition to our vocabulary, its roots run deep in history. Jacob's story highlights how individuals have long grappled with the importance of their personal reputation. The notion that one's name — their identity — carries significant weight and influences how they are perceived has been ingrained in human consciousness for centuries.

In today's world, where personal branding has become a popular buzzword, Jacob's narrative serves as a reminder of the enduring significance of personal reputation and identity. It underscores that the quest for a positive personal brand is not merely a passing trend but a timeless pursuit that transcends cultural and historical boundaries.

HARMONIZING YOUR CORE 4

In this chapter, we covered the concept of personal branding, recognizing that each of us is a brand with unique attributes, values, and perceptions. Understanding you are a brand is aligned with the Mind or Intellectual core, emphasizing the importance of self-awareness, clarity of purpose, and strategic thinking in shaping your personal brand.

To strengthen your Intellectual core, embark on a journey of self-discovery. Take time for introspection to discern your values, strengths, and aspirations. This self-awareness becomes the foundation upon which you build your personal brand.

Craft a strategic roadmap for your personal brand. This involves setting clear goals, defining your unique selling proposition, and aligning your actions and behaviors with the brand you wish to portray to the world.

CHAPTER 3

Principle 3: Come Up With A Plan

"Without vision you're doomed to fail." Proverbs 29:18

When it comes to achieving goals and finding fulfillment, intentional planning plays a pivotal role in the journey. It's the difference between merely moving forward and making significant progress. Purposeful planning involves assembling three crucial elements: understanding the "why" behind your actions, defining your destination, and charting the path that will lead you there.

Just as you wouldn't embark on a voyage without a compass or set out on a road trip without a destination in mind, navigating life without deliberate planning can leave you drifting aimlessly, lacking direction towards your aspirations.

Throughout this chapter, we'll delve into the essence of purposeful planning. We'll unpack Simon Sinek's profound concept of "Start with Why," explore the importance of envisioning your future, and emphasize crafting a mission statement aligned with your core values.

YOUR WHY

Understanding your "why," fostering personal growth, and realizing your aspirations is no easy feat. It often stands as a formidable challenge, one that has personally held me back for years. In fact, this very book is a result of my journey towards uncovering my why.

Unveiling your "why" requires peeling back layers of self-discovery, grappling with questions that may not yield immediate answers. It involves delving into the depths of your being, confronting uncertainties, and embracing the discomfort of introspection. This journey is not a leisurely stroll; it's a courageous exploration through uncharted terrain, navigating the complexities of your inner landscape.

Many falter along this path, never fully understanding their motivations, values, or deeper aspirations. This elusive "why" becomes the missing puzzle piece in the picture of their lives—a void that, when left unaddressed, can hinder progress and fulfillment.

Yet, despite its challenges, the rewards are immense. Discovering your "why" acts as the compass that guides you towards your true purpose, aligning your actions with your core values and aspirations. It's the foundation upon which a life of authenticity, purpose, and fulfillment is built. As Mark Twain famously said, "The two most important days of your life are the day you are born, and the day you find out why."

In the chapters ahead, I invite you to confront this challenge head-on. While the journey may be daunting and the waters may be deep and cold, I encourage you to dive in courageously. Together, we'll navigate the depths of understanding your "why," paving the way for a life of purpose and resonance.

Exploring Simon Sinek's "Start with Why"

Navigating through the abundance of personal growth resources can indeed be overwhelming, with a plethora of books, videos, and courses vying for your attention. Amidst this sea of information, Simon Sinek's concept of "Start with Why" emerges as a guiding light. Through his influential book and TED Talk, Sinek delves into the essence of motivation and purpose, challenging you to uncover the fundamental reasons behind your actions and aspirations.

At its core, "Start with Why" emphasizes that understanding the "why" behind your endeavors is paramount. Sinek suggests that this intrinsic motivation is more critical than the "what" or "how" of your pursuits. Indeed, the "why" serves as the bedrock of inspiration, propelling you towards success.

· "Start with Why" transcends professional and personal boundaries, serving as a guiding principle for influencers, businesses, and individuals alike. It prompts you to consider the significance of your existence and the resonance of your goals with your innermost being.

In the context of your personal growth journey, "Start with Why" serves as a cornerstone. It invites you to peel back the layers of your existence, revealing the essence of your motivations. This introspection ignites the flame of purpose within you, setting the stage for a profound exploration of self-discovery and fulfillment.

Diving Deeper Into Purposeful Planning

Let's go just a tad bit deeper into the power of purposeful planning and explore various methodologies and frameworks that can serve as invaluable tools in organizing your thoughts and actions effectively. While the concept of planning may seem straightforward, the approaches you take can significantly impact the clarity, efficiency, and success of your endeavors.

In this section, I'll introduce you to a diverse array of planning methodologies and frameworks, each offering unique perspectives and strategies to help you chart your course towards your goals. Whether you're embarking on a personal journey of growth, launching a new project, or leading a team towards a common vision, having the right planning framework can make all the difference.

From traditional strategic planning models to innovative agile methodologies, I'll cover a spectrum of approaches tailored to different contexts and objectives. By understanding these methodologies and selecting the most suitable ones for your needs, you can enhance your ability to navigate complexities, overcome obstacles, and achieve meaningful outcomes.

So, let's explore the world of planning methodologies and frameworks, equipping you with the knowledge and tools to plan with purpose and precision.

Here's an overview of some commonly used planning methodologies tailored to personal improvement:

1. **SMART Goals:** SMART is an acronym for **S**pecific, **M**easurable, **A**chievable, **R**elevant, and **T**ime-bound. This methodology focuses on setting clear and concise goals that are well-defined, quantifiable, attainable, relevant to one's aspirations, and bound by a deadline. SMART goals provide a structured framework for goal-setting and help individuals clarify their objectives, track progress, and stay motivated.

2. **SWOT Analysis:** SWOT stands for **S**trengths, **W**eaknesses, **O**pportunities, and **T**hreats. This technique involves identifying and evaluating internal strengths and weaknesses, as well as external opportunities and threats. By conducting a SWOT analysis, individuals can gain insights into their unique strengths and weaknesses, uncover potential opportunities for growth, and identify potential obstacles or challenges to overcome.

3. **Personal Development Plan (PDP):** A Personal Development Plan is a structured framework for setting personal and professional development goals. It typically includes an assessment of current skills, strengths, and areas for improvement, as well as specific objectives and action plans to achieve them. A PDP provides a roadmap for personal growth and development, helping individuals enhance their skills, capabilities, and performance.

4. **Life Wheel:** The Life Wheel is a visual tool used to assess and balance different areas of life, such as career, relationships, health, finances, and personal growth. By evaluating each area and assigning a rating based on

satisfaction or fulfillment, individuals can identify areas of imbalance and prioritize areas for improvement. The Life Wheel helps individuals create a holistic view of their life and develop strategies to achieve balance and harmony.

5. Mind Mapping: Mind mapping is a creative technique for organizing thoughts, ideas, and goals visually. It involves creating a visual representation of interconnected concepts, using branches and nodes to illustrate relationships and associations. Mind mapping can be used to brainstorm ideas, clarify goals, and develop action plans. It encourages creative thinking, enhances problem-solving skills, and improves memory and retention.

6. Kaizen: Kaizen, which means "continuous improvement" in Japanese, is a philosophy and methodology focused on making small, incremental changes over time to achieve continuous improvement. It emphasizes the importance of ongoing learning, experimentation, and adaptation. By adopting a Kaizen mindset, individuals can develop habits of continuous learning, growth, and improvement in all aspects of life.

These planning methodologies offer different approaches to personal improvement, each with its own strengths and applications. By understanding and utilizing these methodologies effectively, individuals can develop clear goals, create actionable plans, and make progress towards their aspirations. To learn more about any of them simply do an internet search and you'll find a plethora of information about each of them.

You've Been Bamboozled

Ever pondered why birds instinctively migrate from north to south? It's because it's encoded in their very essence—a compass guiding their journey through life. Similarly, I believe each of us arrives on this Earth with an innate purpose. At birth, we're intimately connected with this programming, an unfiltered understanding of our direction.

Yet, life's intricacies often serve to unravel this programming. How? Enter the "stupid people" we discussed in Chapter 1—the naysayers of life, often those closest to us. They're the ones consistently dictating what we should or shouldn't do.

Don't allow these 'stupid people' to disrupt your focus. Their sole agenda is to hoodwink and bamboozle you, aiming to derail you from your innate programming. The more you lend them your ear, the more you engage in argument with them, the more likely it is that you'll lose touch with your purpose—the very core that once guided your path.

Just like those migrating birds, you likely have a whisper of desire within you, a calling that resonates, guiding your way. But amid life's clamor, this whisper can fade. It's akin to being deprogrammed, losing touch with your innate motivations.

Reconnecting demands an inward journey—relearning to listen to that calling, rediscovering our innate purpose. It's about recognizing and trusting the inner compass. This pursuit demands knowledge, courage, and skill—a journey of self-discovery and self-mastery.

Let's navigate the tightrope of your "why." Ahead, you'll learn to push through the noise, distractions, and deprogramming. By reconnecting with your inner calling, you can align your actions and aspirations, steering your life toward fulfillment and resonance with your innate purpose. Consider Mozart: at three years old, before he could read or write, he sat down at a piano and began to play with the keys. The piano spoke to him and he to it. They communicated on an organic level, and at eight years old, he wrote his first symphony. How? Because the programming was there before he even emerged from his mother's womb.

Vision vs Mission

Vision and mission are often mistaken for one another, so let's clarify each with a simple definition—a brain tattoo, if you will.

Vision: Where you want to go.

Mission: Why you want to go there.

Pick Yourself For Success

For instance, my personal vision is to inspire people to do the things that inspire them. My mission is to do work that matters for people who care.

So, where am I trying to go every day? To do something in some way that will inspire people. And why do I do these things? Because I want to do work that matters for people who care.

Crafting your vision is like charting a roadmap for your life's journey. It's about setting sail toward a destination that resonates with your soul, even if you need to navigate without a physical map.

It's important to understand that vision has nothing to do with sight—Stevie Wonder proved that. As you get to know me, you'll find that music plays a big part in my thinking and reflection on life. I tell folks I'm a TruFunk Soldier! And as such, Stevie's album "Innervisions" is a personal favorite. In this classic, considered one of the fifty best albums of all time, Stevie sings about the visions that live inside of us. So, ask yourself: What vision lives inside of you? Where are you trying to go? Where are you trying to take your business, your family, your community, the world? What are your innervisions? What's the melody that resonates deep within your soul?

Helen Keller once remarked that the only thing worse than being blind is having sight but no vision. It's a reminder that mere existence isn't enough—it's the vision that breathes life into our endeavors, propelling us toward significance and purpose.

Examples of exemplary vision statements

Bruce Lee:

"I, Bruce Lee, will be the first highest-paid Oriental superstar in the United States. In return, I will give the most exciting performances and render the best quality in the capacity of an actor. Starting in 1970, I will achieve world fame, and from then onward till the end of 1980, I will have in my possession $10,000,000. I will live the way I please and achieve inner harmony and happiness." This vision statement outlines Bruce Lee's specific and measurable goals for his career and personal life.

Steve Jobs:

"To make a dent in the universe." Jobs' vision statement encapsulated his aspiration to create groundbreaking innovations that would revolutionize industries and impact lives globally.

Mother Teresa:

"To give comfort, love, and care to the abandoned, sick, and dying." Mother Teresa's vision statement embodies her life's dedication to serving humanity.

Walt Disney:

"To make people happy, entertain, and bring joy to families through imaginative experiences." Disney's vision centers on spreading joy and happiness through imaginative storytelling.

Maya Angelou:

"To inspire, empower, and uplift through my words, actions, and teachings." Angelou's vision was centered on using her words and actions to uplift and inspire generations.

Oprah Winfrey:

"To use media as a platform for education, inspiration, and positive change in the lives of individuals worldwide." Oprah's vision focused on utilizing media to inspire and positively impact the lives of people globally.

Sonia Sotomayor:

"To promote justice, fairness, and equality through my role as a Supreme Court Justice and public advocate." Sotomayor's vision emphasizes her commitment to upholding justice and equality in her role as a justice and public advocate.

These vision statements from influential individuals offer glimpses into their life's missions, showcasing the power of clear and impactful vision statements in guiding decisions and actions.

How To Craft Your Vision Statement

Step 1: Reflect on Your Values and Passions

Begin by reflecting on your core values, beliefs, and passions. Consider what truly matters to you and what drives you to take action.

Ask yourself questions such as:

What do I value most in life?

What am I passionate about?

What impact do I want to make in the world?

Take some time to journal or brainstorm ideas related to your values and passions.

Step 2: Envision Your Ideal Future

Close your eyes and imagine your ideal future. Visualize yourself living a fulfilling and meaningful life, aligned with your values and passions.

Consider various aspects of your life, including career, relationships, health, personal development, and community involvement.

Think about the specific goals you want to achieve, and the impact you want to have on yourself and others.

Step 3: Define Your Long-Term Goals

Based on your reflections and vision, define your long-term goals. These are the overarching objectives that you aim to accomplish over the next several years.

Make your goals specific, measurable, achievable, relevant, and time-bound (SMART). For example, instead of saying, "I want to make a difference," specify how you plan to make a difference and by when.

Step 4: Identify Key Themes and Patterns

Review your reflections, vision, and long-term goals to identify key themes and patterns that emerge. Look for recurring ideas, values, or aspirations that resonate with you.

Pay attention to words or phrases that evoke strong emotions or feelings of alignment with your purpose.

Step 5: Draft Your Vision Statement

Use the insights from your reflections, vision, and goals to draft your vision statement. Your vision statement should encapsulate your ultimate destination and aspirations in a few impactful words.

Keep your vision statement concise, clear, and inspiring. Aim for a statement that is memorable and easy to understand.

Consider using a template or framework to structure your vision statement. Here's a simple template to follow:

"My vision is to [verb] [noun] [outcome] by [action]."

For example, "My vision is to inspire lifelong learning and personal growth by empowering individuals to pursue their passions and unleash their full potential."

Step 6: Refine and Revise Your Vision Statement

Once you've drafted your vision statement, take some time to refine and revise it. Consider whether it accurately captures your aspirations and resonates with your values and passions.

Seek feedback from trusted friends, family members, or mentors to ensure your vision statement effectively communicates your intentions.

Edit your vision statement as needed to make it more compelling, concise, and aligned with your goals.

Step 7: Finalize Your Vision Statement

After refining your vision statement, finalize it by ensuring it reflects your authentic self and aligns with your long-term goals.

Write down your vision statement in a prominent place where you can see it regularly, such as on a vision board, sticky note, or digital wallpaper.

Use your vision statement as a guiding light to inspire and motivate you on your journey toward achieving your goals and living a purposeful life.

By following these steps and incorporating brainstorming exercises, template examples, and editing tips, you can effectively craft a vision statement that serves as a powerful guidepost for your personal and professional endeavors.

Harmonizing Your Core 4

Chapter 3 introduced the pivotal concept of crafting a plan, a compass directing your actions toward achieving success. Coming up with a plan resonates strongly with the Mind or Intellectual core, fostering strategic thinking, and goal-setting, allowing you to steer your life's trajectory intentionally.

For better clarity of purpose try to define your objectives clearly. Just as a business plan delineates goals and strategies, outlining your personal aspirations provides a roadmap for progress and growth.

Take time to develop a strategic plan to achieve your goals. Consider breaking down your objectives into manageable steps, creating a clear path forward. This strategic approach nurtures your intellectual abilities and aids in thoughtful decision-making.

A robust plan isn't rigid but adaptable. Embrace flexibility in your planning, allowing room for adjustments as circumstances change. This adaptability ensures your plan remains relevant and aligned with your evolving aspirations.

By integrating strategic planning into your life, you're nurturing your Intellectual or Mind core, enhancing your ability to strategize, plan, and adapt. This synchronization among the Core 4 components empowers you to design a life that aligns with your deepest ambitions.

Pick Yourself For Success

CHAPTER 4

PRINCIPLE 4: CONFRONT CHALLENGES

"We choose to go to the moon in this decade and do the other things, not because they are easy, but because they are hard." - President John F. Kennedy

President John F. Kennedy said, "We choose to go to the moon in this decade and do the other things, not because they are easy, but because they are hard." This sentiment strikes right at the heart of what it means to contend—the willingness to face challenges head-on, not for the sake of ease, but for the pursuit of greatness.

Sometimes I wonder what my life as an African American would be like if Rosa Parks, Dr. King, Bayard Rustin, or any of the lesser known civil rights leaders had decided that the battle was just too hard and given up. You see, when you make a choice to do the hard thing sometimes things might not get better for you but they will get better for the generation that follows.

In the journey of life, the path of least resistance often calls out, offering the allure of ease and comfort. Yet, hidden within the folds of this seemingly effortless route lies a paradox: the choice between temporary comfort and lasting fulfillment.

This paradox underlines a profound truth about the nature of challenges and their pivotal role in shaping our destinies. The inclination to avoid difficulty is ingrained within us, steering us away from the strenuous, the demanding, and the arduous. However, the very essence of growth, success, and contentment often resides in contending with the difficult.

In this chapter, I want to bring you head to head with the notion that embracing the hard things is not merely an option but a necessity on the road to fulfillment. Together we'll explore the transformative power embedded within the discomfort of facing challenges and the rewards that await those who dare to tread the path less traveled. Let's get ready to rumble and explore the idea of accepting adversity.

Invictus

"Invictus" by William Ernest Henley is one of my favorite poems. I first encountered it in college, and its message has stayed with me ever since. It serves as a reminder of the wisdom my mother imparted to me in my childhood, before life stripped away its innocence. She used to say, in her deep southern accent, "what don't kill ya, will sho' God strengthen ya." At the time, I didn't fully grasp its meaning, but now I understand: overcoming hardship makes us stronger in the long run.

A closer look at "Invictus."

"Out of the night that covers me,

Black as the pit from pole to pole,

I thank whatever gods may be

For my unconquerable soul."

These opening lines acknowledge the darkness and challenges that surround us. Despite these difficulties, they celebrate the inner strength and resilience inherent in the human spirit. This resonates with the core message of this book, emphasizing the importance of recognizing and appreciating our unconquerable nature as we strive for success.

"In the fell clutch of circumstance

Pick Yourself For Success

I have not winced nor cried aloud.

Under the bludgeonings of chance

My head is bloody, but unbowed."

Henley's words here embody the attitude toward adversity—despite facing relentless challenges, the resolve to persevere and stand firm remains unshaken. This aligns perfectly with the essence of the Pick Yourself For Success spirit, emphasizing the importance of facing hard things without faltering, acknowledging the struggles yet remaining resolute.

"Beyond this place of wrath and tears

Looms but the Horror of the shade,

And yet the menace of the years

Finds and shall find me unafraid."

This verse speaks of courage in the face of hardships, acknowledging the presence of darkness beyond immediate challenges. It reminds us that to reach our desired destination, we must move beyond our current struggles, confront future uncertainties with courage, and refuse to succumb to fear despite the unknown.

"...I am the master of my fate, I am the captain of my soul."

These last two lines reflect the essence of empowerment and self-determination. They serve as a rallying call for the pick yourself for success tribe—

to fully embrace the idea that you can and must Pick Yourself For Success. These words emphasize the control you as an individual hold over your destiny. All successful people understand this power—they navigate their lives, take charge, and steer themselves toward success by contending with life's challenges. While faith plays a part, as my favorite book says, "faith without work is dead."

Why Do Hard Things

Have you ever watched a professional long distance bike ride like the Tour De France? If you pay close attention to the bikes, you'll spot an interesting fact: all the bike seats are the hard type, without any cushion. Why? Because professional cyclists understand that hard seats provide better support and prevent discomfort in the long run.

Human nature often leads you to avoid challenging tasks, seeking comfort even in simple endeavors, such as opting for a cushy bike seat when riding. That's why casual riders tend to prefer gel-based, comfortable saddles, while professionals choose hard, unpadded seats for extended rides.

Soft seats may offer immediate comfort but can cause discomfort over time due to rubbing and chafing. Conversely, hard seats may seem uncomfortable at first but provide lasting support, leading to increased comfort during extended rides. This analogy mirrors your experiences in life.

Pick Yourself For Success

In various aspects of life, including careers and relationships, the easy path often beckons. Yet, tackling challenges head-on fosters emotional resilience and strengthens character, leading to long-term growth. President Kennedy's speech exemplifies this, emphasizing the value of facing difficulty in pursuit of monumental goals.

Confronting hard tasks, whether in personal growth or professional endeavors, enhances your ability to navigate life's complexities. Similar to how professional cyclists benefit from hard seats for smoother rides, embracing challenges equips you to handle life's ups and downs with greater ease in the long run.

POWER TIP
Successful people have learned to be comfortable being uncomfortable.

THE WALL

"So wide you can't get around it. So low you can't get under it. So high you can't get over it." "Here's your chance to dance your way out of your constriction." - George Clinton

"**The Wall**" is a formidable obstacle, a challenge encountered by marathon runners where fatigue and mental exhaustion converge, testing their willpower. Yet, in life's marathon, encountering your own wall is inevitable. It's not a matter of if but when. And when that moment arrives, you must summon the determination to overcome, surpass, circumvent, or break through it.

Legendary funk-master George Clinton once sang, *"So wide you can't get around it, so low you can't get under it, so high you can't get over it. But here's your chance to dance your way out of your constriction."* These lyrics capture life's challenges, highlighting obstacles that seem impassable, restricting, or overwhelming.

Consider what constricts you in life. Reflect on the barriers—whether mental, emotional, or circumstantial—that confine your progress or hinder your endeavors. Is it fear, self-doubt, external pressures, or limiting beliefs that create these walls?

I, too, have faced my own personal, professional, and financial walls. Professionally, I navigated the ups and downs of being laid off or downsized three times. On the personal front, at forty-five years old I heard the three most feared words, "you have cancer." Financially, my wife and I weathered the storm of the 2007 - 2009 recession, spending over $250,000 of our retirement savings.

Each time I hit those walls, it demanded a hard reset—a recalibration of perspectives, an unwavering commitment to push through, and a readiness to rebuild from the ground up. Hitting these walls wasn't the end; it marked the beginning of a renewed resolve, an opportunity to reframe challenges, and a chance to discover unforeseen strengths.

Similar to a marathoner facing the wall, confronting life's constraints requires a shift in mindset—a resolve to find ways around the barriers, a determination to metaphorically dance out of your constriction. It's about channeling resilience and creativity, seeking alternative paths, and summoning the courage to break free from what confines you.

Remember, hitting the wall isn't a sign of failure; it's an inevitable part of the journey. It's what you do when you hit that wall that defines your path forward. Embrace the challenge, acknowledge the barriers, and seize the opportunity to navigate your way past them. These constraints are not roadblocks but invitations to discover your inner strength and resourcefulness.

GET COMFORTABLE BEING UNCOMFORTABLE

I once heard celebrity fitness trainer Jillian Michaels say that if you want to change your body, you need to become comfortable being uncomfortable. It struck a chord with me and has stayed with me ever since. The truth is, this principle applies to change in any aspect of life. Stepping into discomfort is a crucial step toward transformation and growth. Often, it means embracing uncomfortable conversations, both with oneself and with others.

Rodney Goldston

Consider addressing poor performance or behavior in the workplace—it's uncomfortable for both parties, yet essential for improvement. Similarly, in personal relationships, confronting a partner or family member about something that needs to change can be extremely challenging.

Let's face it: change makes people uncomfortable. It requires challenging norms, facing hard truths, and questioning ingrained beliefs. However, it's in these uncomfortable spaces that growth happens. So, get used to saying to yourself and to others, "This is going to be uncomfortable," as it often precedes significant breakthroughs.

Allow me to share an analogy from the world of fitness, as I used to be quite the gym enthusiast. Imagine you can do ten bicep curls with twenty pounds. Do you know which repetition gives you the most benefit? It's not the fifth or the tenth. It's the eleventh —the one that hurts the most. The one where you've pushed past your physical and mental limit challenges your muscle fiber to adapt and grow stronger.

On May 25, 2020, Americans were thrust into a profoundly uncomfortable conversation. The murder of George Floyd, an African American man, by a white police officer, captured on video by a bystander, forced the nation into a necessary but uncomfortable dialogue. It became a catalyst for discussions about systemic racism, police brutality, and social justice. The discomfort it generated led to widespread protests, demanding accountability and prompting introspection into deeply rooted societal issues.

Pick Yourself For Success

This tragic incident compelled individuals and communities to confront uncomfortable truths about racial inequality, sparking conversations about privilege, bias, and the urgent need for societal reforms. The discomfort it caused propelled movements advocating for accountability, equality, and systemic change.

The uncomfortable conversations and revelations stemming from George Floyd's murder highlight that change often arises from discomfort. They underscore the importance of engaging with uncomfortable truths to initiate meaningful transformation and progress.

In addition to the discomfort sparked by events like George Floyd's murder, another powerful example is the #MeToo movement. This movement forced the nation to confront an uncomfortable truth about the pervasive issue of sexual harassment and assault, particularly in the workplace. Women bravely shared their experiences, often facing stigma and backlash, but their courage ignited a global conversation about gender inequality and power dynamics.

Similar to the discomfort experienced in discussions about race and social justice, the conversations prompted by #MeToo were uncomfortable but necessary. They shed light on systemic issues, challenged societal norms, and pushed for accountability and change. The discomfort of confronting these uncomfortable truths propelled movements advocating for gender equality, workplace reform, and cultural shifts in attitudes towards women.

By acknowledging the discomfort of addressing issues like racism, sexism, and sexual harassment, we recognize that growth often emerges from these uncomfortable spaces. It's through these difficult conversations and confrontations that individuals and society as a whole can evolve and progress towards a more just and equitable future.

Asking yourself what the most difficult thing you can do today is—and then doing it—will push you beyond your comfort zones. It's in these uncomfortable spaces that you will find the most profound growth, change, and ultimately, success.

Remember, embracing discomfort, in whatever form it arises, is often the path to profound personal and social evolution.

Gettn' Gritty Wit' It

In Angela Duckworth's book "Grit," she delves into the power of passion and perseverance as crucial elements for achieving long-term goals. The concept of getting gritty perfectly aligns with embracing challenges with determination and resilience.

Reading Duckworth's insights was uncomfortable yet enlightening for me. It forced me to confront a truth about myself—I lacked grit. I had walked away from numerous challenges simply because they became too difficult. Recognizing this discomfort was a turning point. Remember earlier when I wrote about getting comfortable being uncomfortable? To improve, I had to face uncomfortable truths about my lack of perseverance in some areas of my life.

Life often presents tough hurdles, requiring a gritty attitude—an unwavering commitment to overcoming obstacles and difficulties. Duckworth's research emphasizes that success isn't solely determined by natural talent but also by sustained effort, resilience, and what she defines as grit. As I like to say, "Hard work will outwork talent when talent won't work." This means that while there may be plenty of individuals more talented and gifted than you, sometimes they falter due to laziness, allowing hard work (grit) to prevail.

The connection between grit and facing hard things is profound. It's about more than just enduring challenges; it's about approaching them with unwavering determination and tenacity. Similar to the final, grueling repetition in weightlifting, developing grit requires exercising one's perseverance muscles.

Gettn' Gritty Wit' It isn't about shying away from difficulty; it's about confronting it head-on with dedication and persistence. It's the commitment to consistently take on hard tasks, refusing to settle for mediocrity or the easy way out.

So, when faced with daunting tasks, embrace your inner grit and get gritty wit' it. Approach challenges with determination and resilience, embodying the spirit of getting gritty highlighted by Duckworth's research. Gettn' Gritty Wit' It isn't merely a phrase; it's a mindset—a dedication to tackling hard things with passion, perseverance, and an unyielding determination to conquer obstacles.

STRATEGIES FOR OVERCOMING ADVERSITY

The power to shape your destiny resides within you. - Rodney Goldston

Life is a journey filled with both triumphs and tribulations. From the mundane challenges of daily life to the devastating blows that leave us shaken to our core, we are constantly tested by the unpredictable nature of existence. Just as the sun rises and sets, so too do you encounter moments of joy and sorrow, success and failure.

In the midst of life's trials, your proverbial walls, it is easy to feel overwhelmed by the weight of your challenges, questioning whether you have the courage to endure. I remember a particularly sad moment when this reality hit home for me. It was just before I sat down to write this chapter, and I found myself transfixed by a documentary on the 2021 school shooting in Uvalde, Texas. The heart-wrenching accounts of loss and grief left me speechless, grappling with the enormity of such senseless tragedy.

Pick Yourself For Success

In moments like these, it is natural to feel a sense of despair, to wonder how you can find the strength to carry on. Yet, it is precisely during these moments of adversity that the true depth of the human spirit is revealed.

As Dr. Martin Luther King Jr. once said, "We must accept finite disappointment, but never lose infinite hope." In carving hope out of a mountain of despair, you tap into a reservoir of strength that lies within you. Like Nelson Mandela, who emerged from 27 years of imprisonment to lead his nation toward reconciliation and unity. Like J.K. Rowling, who turned rejection into inspiration and became one of the most beloved authors of our time. Like Stephen Hawking, who defied the limitations of his body to explore the mysteries of the universe. And like Bethany Hamilton, who lost her left arm in a shark attack but continued to pursue her passion for surfing with unwavering determination.

These stories teach that hardships are the stepping stones to your greatness. These individuals faced seemingly insurmountable odds and emerged victorious.

A poem that resonates deeply with me is one by Edgar Albert Guest, which speaks to the indomitable spirit that resides within each and every one of us:

"When you're up against trouble,

Meet it squarely face to face;

Rodney Goldston

Lift your chin and set your shoulders

Plant your feet and take a brace.

When it's vain to try and dodge it,

Do the best that you can do;

You may fail, but you may conquer,

See it through!

Black may be the clouds about you

And your future may seem grim,

But don't let your nerve desert you;

Keep yourself in fighting trim.

If the worst is bound to happen,

Spite of all that you can do,

Running from it will not save you

See it through!

Even hope may seem but futile,

When with troubles you're beset

But remember you are facing

Just what other men have met.

You may fail but fall still fighting;

Don't give up what'er you do;

Pick Yourself For Success

Eyes front, head high to the finish.

See it through!"

This poem, first published in 1917 during a period marked by the extreme hardships of World War I, serves to remind us that even in our darkest hour, there is hope, and that we need perseverance in the face of adversity.

5 THINGS YOU CAN DO TO FORTIFY YOURSELF AGAINST THE RISING TIDE OF ADVERSITY

1. BELIEVE IT'S POSSIBLE

When life seems disastrous and you can't see the light at the end of the tunnel, when things are going against you and you're doing everything you know how to do but still aren't seeing results, you must retreat inward and say to yourself: it's possible.

For some visualizing how to get from where they are to where they want to be is too much, so they quit. Whatever your dream is just know if it happened for someone else it's possible it can happen for you.

2: IT TAKES PASSION

As you embark on the journey toward your dreams and aspirations, it's essential to recognize the vital role that passion plays in driving you forward. Passion is not merely a fleeting feeling of excitement; it's a deep, burning desire that fuels your actions and sustains your commitment, even in the face of challenges.

When you're passionate about something, you approach it with unwavering dedication and enthusiasm. It becomes more than just a goal; it becomes a calling—a purpose that ignites your soul and propels you toward your vision of success.

Passion is what separates those who merely exist from those who truly thrive. It's the driving force behind every great achievement, inspiring individuals to push beyond their limits and pursue excellence relentlessly.

3. Take Immediate Action

But passion alone is not enough. It must be coupled with action—a willingness to roll up your sleeves and put in the hard work necessary to turn your dreams into reality. As you strive to reinvent yourself and create the life you envision, remember that passion without action is merely a dream. It's the consistent effort and dedication that transforms passion into progress.

4: It's Up To You

In your journey toward success and fulfillment, one fundamental truth must be acknowledged: the power to shape your life lies squarely within your own hands. It's a pervasive myth in American culture that you are entitled to a great life—that someone other than you is responsible for our perpetual happiness. However, the reality, as the very title of this book suggests, is that there is only one person accountable for the quality of the life you lead, and that person is you.

You must embrace the principle of taking 100% responsibility for everything you experience in your life. This encompasses the level of your achievements, the results you produce, the quality of your relationships, the state of your health and physical fitness, your income, your debts, your feelings—everything! It's not an easy truth to accept, but it's an undeniable reality that must be confronted.

5. Stop Making Excuses

"Excuses are tools of the incompetent, which create monuments of nothingness. Those who specialize in them are seldom good at anything." - George Washington Carver

This quote underscores the idea that making excuses is a trait associated with incompetence, leading to a lack of accomplishment or progress. It suggests that those who frequently make excuses rarely excel in any endeavor because they allow obstacles to stand in their way rather than overcoming them.

All your outcomes, whether positive or negative, are a direct result of how you respond to the events in your life. While you may not always have control over the circumstances you encounter, you do have control over how you choose to interpret and react to them. This power to respond lies at the core of personal responsibility—the recognition that your thoughts, actions, and decisions ultimately shape your reality.

Power Tip

If you do what is easy, your life will be hard. If you do what is hard, your life will be easy.

Harmonizing Your Core 4

The main message I want you to take away from this chapter is that your brilliance needs resilience. Chapter 4, "Contend," is all about the significance of perseverance and resilience in the pursuit of success. The act of Contending resonates deeply with the Emotional or Heart core, fostering resilience, emotional strength, and fortitude as you navigate life's challenges.

You must learn to cultivate resilience in facing adversities. For example, I was listening to a talk by Robert Kyosaki and he said that business statistics tell us that nine out of ten startups fail. Some people read that and decide it's too risky to start, successful entrepreneurs read the same thing and intuitively know they just need to be willing to fail nine times.

Pick Yourself For Success

Learn to see failure as a compass guiding you through the labyrinth of success. Each setback becomes a stepping stone, offering invaluable lessons and resilience. In the dance of trial and error, refine your strategies, cultivate adaptability, and ultimately pave the way for the triumph that springs from the seeds of failure. To learn more about why failure needs to be an option, check out my YouTube video: "Why Failure Must Be An Option."

CHAPTER 5

PRINCIPLE 5: ELEVATE YOUR MIND

"Free your mind and all else will follow." - Rodney Goldston

Freeing your mind is a simple truth. Once that happens, your mind, heart, and body can't help but follow suit.

But how do you go about freeing, or elevating your mind? You start by shifting your paradigm.

The term "paradigm" originates from the Greek word "paradeigma," meaning "pattern" or "example." Essentially, your paradigm is your typical way of thinking—it's your set of beliefs, values, and assumptions that shape how you perceive and understand the world. In short, it's the lens through which you view reality. Or, as Morpheus put it in The Matrix, "It's the world that's been pulled over your eyes to blind you from the truth." And what's the truth? It's that greatness resides within you.

A paradigm shift isn't just a small tweak in your thinking; it's a seismic change in perspective. When Albert Einstein introduced his theory of relativity, he didn't merely refine existing laws of physics; he completely upended them, revolutionizing our understanding of time and space.

Oprah Winfrey didn't just host a talk show—she transformed the entire genre, turning tabloid TV into a platform for meaningful conversations and empowerment. Her paradigm shift elevated talk shows to spaces of inspiration and enlightenment, challenging the conventional notion of success in talk show hosting.

Mahatma Gandhi wasn't just a freedom fighter; he challenged an entire empire's paradigm of power. Through nonviolent resistance, he ushered in a new era of peaceful protest, influencing movements like the American Civil Rights movement led by Dr. Martin Luther King Jr.

Steve Jobs, arguably the greatest businessperson of the 21st century, didn't settle for inventing gadgets; he redefined our relationship with technology, envisioning a world where computers seamlessly integrated into our lives. Jobs' paradigm shift created an ecosystem where innovation and user experience were paramount, revolutionizing multiple industries.

And then there's Muhammad Ali, whose claim to fame was "I float like a butterfly and sting like a bee." Ali transcended sports, laying the groundwork for future athletes to make broader societal impacts. His courage, activism, and career navigation became a blueprint for athletes and creative artists alike.

REFLECT ON THEIR STORIES:

Gandhi's simple life and unwavering commitment to non-violent resistance inspired millions to challenge the vast British Empire. His story shows the power of conviction and moral courage, even against seemingly insurmountable odds.

Ali's victories in the ring transcended boxing. He championed racial equality and social justice, becoming a powerful symbol of resistance. His story reminds us that athletes can use their platforms to fight for positive change.

Oprah's rise from poverty and discrimination to become a media mogul shatters stereotypes. She proves that success can be achieved regardless of background. Her story is one of resilience, determination, and the ability to overcome limitations.

Steve Jobs innovative spirit continues to shape the technological landscape, even after his death. His story reminds us of the enduring power of creativity and the potential for individuals to change the world.

Their actions weren't isolated events; they were seismic shifts in how we perceive creativity, courage, risk, resilience, and conviction. They showed us that paradigms aren't fixed—they're ripe for bold challenges.

Shifting your paradigm is exactly like what the Bible instructs us to do in Romans 12:2: "And be not conformed to this world: but be ye transformed by the renewing of your mind, that ye may prove what is that good, and acceptable, and perfect, will of God." (KJV) This verse emphasizes actively transforming your mindset through studying scripture.

It's my hope that you realize you're standing at the epicenter of your own paradigm shift. So let the shaking begin and shift your paradigm.

You've Got Two Minds

Think of your mind as a ship sailing through life's adventures. But who's in charge? Meet the two main players: your conscious and subconscious minds.

Your conscious mind is like the captain of the ship. It's the thinker, the planner. It makes decisions based on logic and reason, steering your ship toward your goals.

Then there's your subconscious mind, which is like the loyal crew. It doesn't think too much; it just follows orders. It's responsible for your habits, beliefs, and automatic reactions.

Sometimes, these two minds don't see eye to eye. Your conscious mind might want one thing, but your subconscious is stuck on something else. It's like the captain saying "go left" while the crew turns right. Philosopher, Greg Caruso explains in his book Free Will And Consciousness that patterns of human behavior may ultimately be due to factors beyond our conscious control.

To get them working together, you can use tricks like positive thinking. Just like training a pet, you can teach your subconscious to follow the same goals as your conscious mind.

For example an article at Harvard Health discusses the concept of habit formation and how it can be influenced by both conscious and subconscious processes. It highlights techniques like repetition and positive reinforcement, which can be used to "train" the subconscious mind to adopt new behaviors that align with our conscious goals.

But watch out for negative influences! They're like sneaky waves that can push your ship off course. Avoiding them is important, just like avoiding rough waters.

Remember, your subconscious doesn't question things—it just believes them. So, if you keep telling yourself excuses, your subconscious will start to believe them, just like Pavlov's dog learned to expect food at the sound of a bell.

So, understand your two minds. By getting them on the same page, you can steer your ship toward success and happiness, sailing smoothly through life's challenges.

POWER TIP
If you tell yourself excuses long enough, you'll believe them.

HARMONIZING YOUR CORE 4

In Chapter 5, "Elevate Your Mind," we explored the pivotal role of personal growth, and expanding your mental horizons. You learned that the world has been pulled over your eyes to hide the truth of your greatness. Elevating Your Mind corresponds closely with the Intellectual or Mind core, emphasizing the significance of continuous learning, mental agility, and expanding knowledge.

Rodney Goldston

Embrace lifelong learning as the cornerstone of your personal growth. Just as a library accumulates volumes of knowledge, feed your mind with continuous learning experiences, broadening your intellectual horizons.

Cultivating adaptive thinking and mental flexibility by embracing diverse perspectives and being open to new ideas will enrich your intellectual landscape, fostering a more agile and versatile mindset.

Always seek to push the boundaries of your intellectual comfort zone. Much like a horizon that extends beyond the eye's reach, continuously seek to broaden your intellectual capacity, exploring new concepts and domains.

By elevating your mind through continual learning and mental agility, you're nurturing your Intellectual or Mind core, fostering a broader and more adaptable mindset crucial for personal and professional growth.

Pick Yourself For Success

CHAPTER 6

PRINCIPLE 6: STOP LIVING YOUR FEARS

"Too many of us are not living our dreams because we are living our fears." – Les Brown

I'm afraid. These two words echo through the chambers of many minds, young and old alike. As a coach, I've heard these words spill from the lips of Ph.D. holders, hesitant to release their work for fear of rejection by their peers. I've listened to college students share their apprehension about choosing their majors, fearing failure if they pursue certain paths. I've coached young men who are afraid to be fathers.

What this has shown me is that people fear lots of stuff. Some people will even unwittingly sabotage themselves due to fear of reaching their own greatness.

Anything you feed will grow and get stronger. Likewise anything you deprive of nourishment will shrink and get weaker. If you allow your fears to overwhelm you then you will become your own worst enemy. So here's what you have to do. Starve your fear, and feed your faith.

Fear is an invisible yet formidable force that often holds us back. It whispers tales of inadequacy, conjures visions of failure, and sows seeds of doubt. Yet, what if I told you that fear, more often than not, is:

FALSE EVIDENCE APPEARING REAL

In moments of trepidation, it's easy to succumb to fear's illusions, mistaking its appearance for reality. But consider this: the faith spoken of in scripture urges us to walk by faith and not by sight. Therefore faith must be - Finding Answers In The Heart.

Fear often thrives in the shadows of uncertainty, feeding on doubts and insecurities. It paints vivid pictures of what might go wrong, crafting elaborate scenarios that paralyze us into inaction. But what if we dared to shine a light on these fears, to dissect them and expose their falsities?

In challenging fear's grip, you might find that its evidence is flimsy, drawn from the canvas of your imagination rather than the contours of reality. This newfound awareness arms you with courage—the kind that emboldens you to confront your fears, to ask questions, and to seek answers.

Faith, on the other hand, resides within you. It's the compass guiding you through the labyrinth of uncertainties. Faith is not blind; it's a deliberate choice to search for answers in the depths of your being, to trust your intuition and the whispers of your heart.

So, when fear comes knocking, threatening to stall your progress or shatter your dreams, remember that it's often a mirage—an illusion masquerading as truth. Lean into faith, seek solace in the wisdom within, and embrace the journey of Finding Answers In The Heart. In doing so, you might just unearth the courage to live beyond fear and step into the realm of your dreams.

Why You're So Afraid Anyway

Fear is deeply ingrained in our nature, a primal instinct designed to protect us from harm. It's an evolutionary remnant—an alarm system that once alerted our ancestors to imminent danger. This instinctual fear is a valuable tool, vital for survival in hazardous situations.

Pick Yourself For Success

However, in the complexities of modern life, fear has taken on different forms—fearfulness and being afraid. Fearfulness is a chronic state of anxiety, a persistent worry about potential dangers lurking around every corner. It's the nagging unease that creeps in even when there's no immediate threat. Being afraid, on the other hand, is a sharp, immediate response to a specific danger, a momentary surge of adrenaline that readies us for action.

Fearfulness paralyzes you, holds you back from taking risks or pursuing your dreams. It's the voice that whispers doubts and insecurities, urging you to stay within your comfort zones. Being afraid, while uncomfortable, can spur you into action, propelling you to make necessary changes or take precautions when faced with genuine risks.

I vividly recall a moment of intense fear when I found myself just a few feet away from a massive bear. It was a stark reminder of the importance of fear in the face of real danger. In that moment, being afraid was the correct response—I knew I couldn't out-run, out-climb, or out-swim the bear. Fortunately, I was able to maintain my composure and move on, unharmed.

Understanding the distinction between fearfulness and being afraid is crucial. Fearfulness is a hindrance, a barrier that limits your potential and stifles growth. It's the voice that tells you you're not capable or worthy of success. Being afraid, however, can be a catalyst for action, a signal that you're facing a genuine threat and need to respond accordingly.

So, why are you stuck? Are you not where you want to be in life or business? Perhaps it's the fearfulness—the chronic worry and self-doubt—that's holding you back. Recognize the difference between being afraid in the moment and the persistent state of fearfulness. Embrace those acute moments of fear as signals of alertness and readiness to tackle challenges head-on.

It's time to recalibrate your relationship with fear—to discern between the useful response of being afraid and the debilitating state of fearfulness. By doing so, you can find the courage to step beyond the boundaries of fear and embrace the unknown with newfound resilience and determination.

COURAGE OVER FEAR

"I'm not fearing any man." - Dr. Martin Luther King, Jr.

In his final speech, "I've Been to the Mountaintop," delivered amidst threats and violence, Dr. Martin Luther King, Jr. declared, "I'm not fearing any man."

Dr. King's resounding words echo the sentiment that courage isn't the absence of fear but the willingness to act despite it. His unwavering commitment to civil rights and justice in the face of immense opposition stands as a testament to the power of action in the presence of fear.

Pick Yourself For Success

Throughout history, countless individuals have demonstrated remarkable bravery by confronting their fears head-on. Their actions speak volumes about the transformative potential of facing fear rather than succumbing to it.

Rosa Parks, often referred to as the "Mother of the Civil Rights Movement," refused to give up her seat on a segregated bus in Montgomery, Alabama. Her simple yet powerful act ignited a movement that challenged racial segregation and inspired generations.

Malala Yousafzai, an advocate for girls' education, was targeted and shot by the Taliban for her outspoken views. Despite facing grave danger, Malala persevered and continued her activism, becoming the youngest Nobel Prize laureate.

Nelson Mandela spent 27 years in prison for his opposition to apartheid in South Africa. Upon his release, he continued his fight for racial equality and reconciliation, serving as a symbol of hope and resilience.

Each of these individuals faced daunting challenges and palpable fear but chose action over retreat. They embody the idea that courage isn't the absence of fear but the triumph over it. It's about acknowledging fear's presence and choosing to move forward despite its grip.

Their stories teach us that taking action doesn't necessarily mean the absence of fear; it's the conscious decision to defy fear's paralyzing effects. It's the resolve to stand tall and resolute, even in the face of uncertainty and trepidation.

History teaches us that people are most courageous when they act despite their fears. By acknowledging the fear but not letting it dictate your actions, you unlock the door to your own bravery, opening a path toward progress, change, and personal growth.

Beyond the Fear

Understanding Our Inner Resistance

"The more scared we are of a work or calling, the more sure we can be that we have to do it." — Steven Pressfield

While the more scared we are of a work or calling, the more sure we can be that we have to do it (Steven Pressfield), understanding the internal roadblocks to action is key. It's not just a battle between two minds, as we discussed previously, but also the influence of a primal part of our brain.

At the core of our desires and ambitions lies a fascinating paradox - a constant clash between what we say we want and the actions we actually take. We articulate our dreams but stumble when it's time to turn them into reality. Why do these barriers keep cropping up between our intentions and actions?

Early in our brain development, the amygdala forms, which plays a crucial role in processing emotions, particularly fear, and influences our survival instincts. This powerful region, often referred to (though outdated in scientific terms) as the "lizard brain," prioritizes immediate safety and gratification. It's not wired for complex logic or long-term plans.

This part of our brain can be a source of the "resistance" that Steven Pressfield talks about in his works - an invisible force that blocks our creativity, undermines our goals, and whispers doubts in our ear. It's that nagging voice saying, "You can't do it," or "Why bother trying?" (In fact, my amygdala keeps chirping, "Who's gonna read your book anyway?")

Our internal contradictions stem from this ongoing battle between our rational, goal-driven mind and the amygdala's focus on primal instincts and survival. This conflict shows up in our actions - we aim for success but stumble in job interviews, dream big but procrastinate, and crave change but stick to old habits.

Pressfield's depiction of resistance as an adversary mirrors this inner conflict. It's the force that fights against our growth, creativity, and progress, fueled by the amygdala's urge for safety and familiarity.

When you see someone unwaveringly focused on their goals, it's impressive. These folks seem untouched by the contradictions that trip up the rest of us - they're the epitome of relentless action.

Understanding this tug-of-war between our rational mind and the influence of the amygdala is crucial. It's the first step in navigating this complex maze of contradictions, helping you devise strategies to overcome resistance and align your actions with your aspirations.

POWER TIP

Your lizard brain is here to stay. Learn to recognize its voice so you can ignore it.

HARMONIZING YOUR CORE 4

In this chapter you learned that you've got to stop living your fears in order to start living your dreams. This chapter's theme aligns with the Emotional or Heart core, emphasizing emotional control, empathy, and understanding.

TIPS TO HELP TO STOP LIVING YOUR FEARS

First, confront fear and embrace it as a guide, not a deterrent. Instead of letting fear hold you back, see it as a compass guiding you through uncharted territories. Acknowledge its presence but refuse to let it dictate your path. Use it as a tool for growth and self-discovery.

Second, foster empathy for yourself and others. Recognize that emotions, including fear, are part of the human experience. By embracing empathy and understanding, you'll nurture emotional resilience and forge deeper connections.

Third, make courageous choices in the face of fear. Just like a climber ascending a daunting peak, confront your fears with courage. Make decisions that align with your aspirations and values, even when fear tries to hold you back.

By addressing fears with empathy, courage, and understanding, you're harmonizing your Emotional or Heart core. This alignment among the Core 4 components fosters emotional resilience and empowers you to navigate life's challenges with courage and compassion.

Just like a climber ascending a daunting peak, confront your fears with courage. Make decisions that align with your aspirations and values, even when fear tries to hold you back.

CHAPTER 7

PRINCIPLE 7: SWEAT

"Exercise is king. Nutrition is queen. Put them together and you've got a kingdom." - Jack LaLanne

Remember the song 'Early In The Morning' by the Gap Band? Well, it turns out they were onto something. Research has confirmed that one of the most effective ways to truly get out of your head is to kickstart your brain by breaking a sweat first thing in the morning. Scientists now understand what athletes and fitness experts have long recognized: there are significant advantages to exercising in the morning. Particularly, the profound impact of morning perspiration can help you transition from being stuck in your thoughts, to experiencing heightened mental clarity and overall well-being.

THE NEUROCHEMISTRY OF PERSPIRATION

When you engage in physical exercise, especially in the morning, your body releases a flood of neurochemicals that have a profound impact on your mood, cognition, and overall mental health. John Ratey, in his groundbreaking book Spark: The Revolutionary New Science of Exercise and the Brain, explores how exercise promotes the release of neurotransmitters like endorphins, dopamine, and serotonin, which are known to induce feelings of euphoria, happiness, and relaxation. Additionally, exercise triggers the production of Brain-Derived Neurotrophic Factor (BDNF), a protein that supports the growth and maintenance of brain cells, enhances cognitive function, and protects against neurodegenerative diseases. This surge in neurochemicals offers a multitude of benefits: improved mood, sharpened focus, increased resilience to stress, and even enhanced learning and memory. So much so, that John Ratey likens BDNF to Miracle-Gro for the brain.

Perspiration early in the morning serves as a powerful catalyst for stepping out of your head and into the present moment. I try to start priming my body for exercise as soon as I wake up, as my feet hit the floor. Usually with a few simple moves like neck rolls, shoulder shrugs, or hip rotations.

In fact, as I write this it's 4:28 AM, and I've already completed a 25-minute workout and drank 16 ounces of lemon water.

MAKING IT A HABIT

Incorporating morning exercise into your daily routine requires discipline and commitment, but the rewards are well worth the effort. Establishing a consistent habit of perspiring early in the morning sets you up for success, both mentally and physically. Whether it's a brisk jog around the neighborhood, a high-intensity interval training session, or a rejuvenating yoga flow, finding an activity that resonates with you and brings joy is key to making morning exercise a sustainable and enjoyable part of your lifestyle.

By embracing the practice of exercising in the morning and harnessing the power of perspiration to step out of your head, you cultivate a profound sense of well-being, resilience, and mental clarity. This empowers you to navigate life's challenges with grace and confidence. So, lace up those sneakers, break a sweat, and witness as your mornings—and your life—transform before your eyes.

While we're on the subject of sweating and exercise, it's worth noting that health and fitness are often used interchangeably, but they represent distinct aspects of your well-being. Health encompasses the overall state of your body and mind, while fitness refers to your physical capabilities and endurance. Understanding this difference is essential as you embark on your journey toward holistic success.

Health and Fitness

Your Health: The Foundation of Well-Being

Health encompasses more than just the absence of illness; it includes your physical, mental, and emotional well-being. Factors such as nutrition, sleep quality, stress management, and mental resilience contribute to overall health. Being healthy means having the energy and vitality to engage fully in life, cope effectively with stress, and maintain a positive outlook.

Your Fitness: Strength and Endurance

Fitness focuses on physical capabilities and performance, including cardiovascular endurance, muscular strength, flexibility, and agility. Being fit involves having the strength, stamina, and mobility to perform physical tasks and activities with ease.

While health and fitness are related, they're distinct concepts. You can be healthy without being fit, and vice versa. For example, you may have excellent overall health but lack physical fitness due to a sedentary lifestyle. Conversely, you might be physically fit but struggle with mental health issues or chronic stress.

Understanding this difference allows you to adopt a holistic approach to well-being. By prioritizing both health and fitness and addressing their unique needs, you can achieve a balanced and sustainable lifestyle that supports your overall health and vitality.

Personal Experience: A Lesson Learned

At age forty-seven I was diagnosed with cancer, a stark wake-up call. Despite feeling physically strong, I was unaware of the life-threatening health condition lurking beneath the surface. This experience taught me that while I may have been fit, I wasn't truly healthy.

Bob Harper: The Picture of Fitness

Bob Harper, renowned for his book "The Skinny Rules," epitomized physical fitness. His best-selling book, chiseled physique, and unwavering dedication to exercise made him a beacon of inspiration for countless fitness enthusiasts. However, in 2017, while working out in the gym, Bob suffered a massive heart attack, challenging the perception of his invincibility. This alarming incident served as a poignant reminder that even individuals seemingly at the peak of fitness can encounter serious health issues.

Following his heart attack, Bob disclosed in interviews that he had been diagnosed with a hereditary condition leading to elevated levels of lipoprotein(a) in his blood. Lipoprotein(a) is associated with cholesterol transport and can contribute to arterial plaque buildup and blood clots, increasing the risk of cardiovascular disease. Like many, Bob discovered that despite his impressive fitness level, he wasn't immune to health challenges.

This story highlights the crucial difference between health and fitness. While fitness pertains to physical capabilities and performance, health encompasses broader aspects of well-being, including mental and emotional dimensions. Understanding and integrating both health and fitness into your wellness regimen can empower you to proactively safeguard your overall well-being and lead a vibrant, fulfilling life.

POWER TIP

Given the myriad of empirical benefits of exercise, why limit yourself to just one workout a day. After a day's work, indulge in an "Encore Effort" session to maximize the advantages of physical activity and enhance your overall health and vitality.

HARMONIZING YOUR CORE 4

In Principle 7, "Sweat," we explored the transformative power of morning perspiration and its profound impact on your well-being. Just as physical exertion invigorates your body, it also resonates deeply with each aspect of your Core 4—your Intellect, Emotion, Spirit, and Physical.

1. Intellect: Engaging in physical exercise stimulates the release of neurotransmitters that enhance cognitive function and mental clarity. Just as expanding your mental horizons elevates your mind, morning sweat nourishes your intellect, sharpening your focus and enhancing your cognitive abilities.

2. Emotion: The euphoria and sense of accomplishment that accompany a morning workout uplift your mood and enhance emotional well-being. Much like cultivating emotional resilience, breaking a sweat in the morning infuses your day with positivity and vitality, empowering you to navigate life's challenges with grace and optimism.

3. Spirit: Morning perspiration connects you to your inner strength and vitality, fostering a sense of spiritual renewal and alignment with your deeper purpose. Just as nurturing your spirit through reflection and mindfulness elevates your soul, embracing physical exertion in the morning awakens your spirit, empowering you to live with intention and purpose.

Sweating in the morning energizes your body, strengthens your muscles, and enhances your overall physical health. Similar to maintaining physical fitness, incorporating morning exercise into your routine nurtures your body, promoting longevity and vitality, and empowering you to lead an active and fulfilling life.

Pick Yourself For Success

By harmonizing your Core 4 through the practice of morning sweat, you're cultivating a holistic sense of well-being that resonates throughout every aspect of your life. Embrace the interconnectedness of your mind, heart, soul, and body, and let the rhythm of morning perspiration guide you toward a life of vitality, purpose, and fulfillment.

CHAPTER 8

The SUCCESS System Review

Congratulations on reaching the end of this section of the book! As you've traversed through the chapters, you might have discerned a subtle pattern—each chapter title is a letter in the acronym of SUCCESS. Let's briefly recap what each stands for:

S - Stupid People. This chapter emphasized the importance of surrounding yourself with individuals and energy conducive to growth.

U - Understand You Are a Brand: Here we explored the concept of personal branding, recognizing yourself as a brand, and nurturing it effectively.

Pick Yourself For Success

C - Come Up With a Plan: Here, we discussed the significance of planning, strategizing, and setting goals to achieve success.

C - Confront Challenges: I urged you to face challenges head-on, confront fears, and persevere despite obstacles to reach your desired destination.

E - Elevate Your Mindset: The chapter focused on the power of mindset, positivity, and personal development in driving success.

S - Stop Living Your Fears: Encouraged you to confront fears that hold you back, emphasizing the need to take calculated risks and overcome limitations.

S - Sweat: The final chapter urged you to embrace physical exertion and morning perspiration as catalysts for personal growth.

Each chapter served as a guidepost on your journey toward personal empowerment, offering insights, strategies, and a roadmap for you to pick yourself up and unleash your potential.

Remember, success is not just an endpoint but an ongoing journey—a pursuit of personal growth, resilience, and continuous improvement. You are now equipped with a toolkit that encourages you to forge your path, embrace your uniqueness, and aspire for greatness.

Now that you've explored the *SUCCESS System* and gained valuable insights into personal empowerment and growth, it's time to delve deeper into the journey of self-discovery and transformation. In the next sections of the book, we will explore two critical aspects of personal development: Stepping Out Of Your Head and Stepping Into Your Greatness. These sections will provide you with practical strategies, mindset shifts, and actionable steps to overcome self-limiting beliefs, unlock your full potential, and live a life of purpose and fulfillment. Get ready to embark on the next phase of your journey, where you'll learn to break free from mental barriers and embrace the greatness that lies within you.

Pick Yourself For Success

SECTION TWO

STEPPING OUT OF YOUR HEAD

CHAPTER 9

How You Got in Your Head?

"You are the master of your destiny. You can influence, direct, and control your own environment. You can make your life what you want it to be." - Napoleon Hill

Imagine a newborn. Their eyes sparkle with curiosity, reaching out to explore the world around them without hesitation. Fearless adventurers, babies haven't learned to second-guess themselves or worry about what others might think. Every experience is an exciting adventure. So, how do we transform from these uninhibited explorers into self-doubting individuals trapped inside our own heads?

Many of us can trace this shift back to the well-meaning, but often misguided, influences of the world around us. From a young age, we're bombarded with messages about limitations: "What you can and cannot achieve," "What's realistic and what's not." Simply telling a child, "be seen and not heard," can be internalized as, "my voice doesn't matter," potentially leading to a diminished sense of self-worth.

SEEDS OF DOUBT AND EXTERNAL INFLUENCES

Whether it's a parent, teacher, or mentor, someone somewhere can plant seeds of doubt in our minds, shaping our beliefs and limiting our potential. Researchers at Indiana University suggests that negative stereotypes can influence performance, particularly in fields where those stereotypes are prevalent. For example, women in science and math fields may experience anxiety or diminished confidence when reminded of the stereotype that "women are bad at math." This can be a temporary phenomenon, but it highlights the power of external influences on our self-belief.

Take, for example, the story of my daughter's journey to college. Despite her stellar academic record and extracurricular achievements, a well-intentioned high school counselor suggested that the University of Pennsylvania might be a "stretch" for her. This single piece of advice, as anecdotal as it may be, illustrates the power external voices can have on our aspirations. Thankfully, months of encouragement from her family helped her defy those expectations. Her acceptance letter, a testament to her resilience and determination, serves as a powerful reminder that we can overcome external doubts.

But Here's the Good News: You Have the Power

The good news is, just because someone plants a seed of doubt doesn't mean you have to let it take root. You have the power to challenge and reshape your beliefs, to break free from the confines of your own mind and pursue your dreams with unwavering confidence.

My Story: A Counterpoint to Doubt

However, it's important to acknowledge the positive influences that can also shape our self-belief. I was incredibly fortunate to have a cadre of teachers in high school who believed in me. They introduced me to the magic of Broadway plays, the power of Shakespeare's words, the world of drama, and the importance of teamwork. These experiences not only ignited a passion for the arts but also instilled in me valuable life lessons.

My support system extended beyond the classroom walls. Growing up in a single-parent home with an absent father, I believe God provided for me through the presence of incredible mentors in my family and community.

In particular, my mother who told me she loved me everyday (she still does this), my all of older cousins, my neighbor David Denny, Sr., and my best friend's father, Edward Gay, Sr., were instrumental figures in my life. They took a genuine interest in me, offered guidance without ever trying to steer me wrong, and always believed in my potential.

Conclusion: Reclaiming Your Power

The narrative of self-doubt doesn't have to be your story. You can reclaim your autonomy, embrace your innate creativity, and chart your own course in life. It starts by recognizing the power of your thoughts and their influence on your actions. By challenging limiting beliefs, surrounding yourself with positive influences, and taking decisive action towards your goals, you can break free from the confines of your own mind and step boldly into your greatness.

Power Tip

Throughout the day, you're bombarded with messages. Identify the ones limiting you and rewrite your story. Surround yourself with positive influences and take action towards your dreams. You are the author of your own destiny.

CHAPTER 10

THE DOMINO EFFECT

"The person on the top of the mountain didn't fall there." - Rodney Goldston

Everything you do, and say has a cascading effect in your life. It's what I like to call the transformative power of the domino effect. Have you ever marveled at the simple yet profound principle behind a line of falling dominos? Each domino, no matter how small, has the potential to set off a chain reaction of events, leading to significant outcomes.

Pick Yourself For Success

Remember Forrest Gump's famous line, "Life is like a box of chocolates, you never know what you're going to get." Well I like to say life is like a game of dominoes. Meaning, much like in the game of dominoes, your actions have a ripple effect—a domino effect—that extends far beyond the initial moment of impact. Yet, too often, you may find yourself paralyzed by self-doubt, fear, and inertia, trapped within the confines of your own mind. You hesitate to take that first step, fearing failure or rejection, and consequently, you miss out on the opportunity to unleash your full potential.

But what if I told you that by toppling just one domino, you could set off a cascade of positive change in your life? What if that one small action could lead to a series of victories, each building upon the last, propelling you forward toward your goals and dreams?

In this section, you'll explore the liberating concept of the domino effect and its profound implications for personal growth and success. You'll learn to identify the barriers that keep you stuck in your head, holding you back from taking action. And most importantly, you'll discover practical strategies for overcoming fear, embracing imperfection, and harnessing the power of momentum to propel you toward your aspirations.

Are you ready to tip the first domino and embark on a path of growth, resilience, and fulfillment? Your journey begins now—step out of your head and into your greatness.

Identifying Barriers

In your journey to unleash your potential and achieve your dreams, it's crucial to identify the barriers that may stand in your way. These barriers can manifest in various forms, often hindering your ability to take action and make progress toward your goals. Let's explore some common barriers that might be holding you back:

1. Fear of Failure: One of the most common barriers is the fear of failure. You might worry about what others might think if you don't succeed, and this fear can keep you stuck in a cycle of inaction.

2. Self-Doubt: Another barrier is self-doubt, which often stems from a lack of confidence in your abilities. You may question whether you're capable of achieving your goals or worry that you'll never be good enough.

3. Perfectionism: Perfectionism is another common barrier that can hold you back. You might set impossibly high standards for yourself and become paralyzed by the fear of making mistakes.

4. Procrastination: Procrastination is the enemy of progress, often preventing you from taking action on your goals. You may put off important tasks until the last minute, allowing distractions and excuses to derail your plans.

As you continue to read this book, especially the section on Stepping Out of Your Head, I will guide you in understanding and working through these barriers. By identifying and acknowledging these obstacles, you can begin to take proactive steps to overcome them and unlock your full potential.

EMBRACING IMPERFECTION

In your journey toward success, it's essential to embrace imperfection and view failure not as a setback, but as an opportunity for growth. Society often glorifies perfection, but the truth is that perfection is unattainable and unrealistic. Instead of striving for perfection, strive for progress and improvement.

Failure is a natural part of the learning process and is necessary for growth and development. Instead of fearing failure, embrace it as a chance to learn, adapt, and grow stronger. Remember the wisdom of Proverbs 24:16, which says, "The righteous may fall seven times and rise again." This verse teaches us that even the most successful individuals face challenges and setbacks but have the resilience to rise above them.

Embracing imperfection also means adopting a growth mindset, which is the belief that your abilities and intelligence can be developed through dedication and hard work. By cultivating a growth mindset, you'll be more resilient in the face of adversity and more willing to take risks and try new things.

So, the next time you encounter failure or setbacks on your journey, remember that it's all part of the process. Embrace imperfection, learn from your mistakes, and keep pushing forward with resilience and determination. With God's strength and grace, you can overcome any obstacle and achieve your dreams.

Harnessing the Domino Effect

In your journey towards success, it's important to recognize the power of overcoming small challenges. Just like a line of falling dominoes, tackling small obstacles can create a ripple effect of momentum and progress in your life. Each small victory builds upon the last, propelling you forward towards your goals and dreams.

Think about it like climbing a mountain. The person at the top didn't fall there; they climbed. They worked hard, step by step, overcoming obstacles along the way. It's like the childhood song from the Christmas movie Santa Claus Is Coming To Town says, "Put One Foot in Front of the Other." Taking that first step is the key to making progress.

Overcoming small challenges is about simply putting one foot in front of the other. It's about taking that first step, or knocking down that first domino. Remember, even the most successful individuals started small and faced challenges along the way.

All successful people have overcome some type of adversity to achieve significant success. People like Oprah Winfrey, who overcame a difficult childhood to become one of the most influential women in the world, or Madam C.J. Walker, who went from poverty to becoming the first female self-made millionaire in America. Their stories are testaments to the power of persistence and resilience in the face of obstacles.

One of the things that separates humans from animals is our ability to overcome our programming. While your difficulties may seem daunting, remember that it all starts with taking that first step. By harnessing the domino effect and overcoming small challenges, you can create momentum and make progress towards your goals.

Action Steps

1. Reflect on Your Barriers: Take some time to identify the barriers that are holding you back from taking action. Is it fear of failure, self-doubt, or something else? Be honest with yourself and write down any thoughts or feelings that come to mind.

2. Challenge Your Mindset: Once you've identified your barriers, challenge them. Ask yourself if these beliefs are serving you or holding you back. Remember, Proverbs 24:16 tells us that the righteous may fall seven times, but they rise again. Adopt a growth mindset and view setbacks as opportunities for growth.

3. Set Specific Goals: Determine what you want to achieve and set specific, measurable goals to get there. Break down your goals into smaller, actionable steps that you can take consistently.

4. Take Small Actions: Start taking small actions towards your goals, even if they seem insignificant. Remember, every small step you take creates momentum and moves you closer to your aspirations.

5. Track Your Progress: Keep track of your actions and progress over time. This could be as simple as journaling or using a goal-tracking app. Celebrate your victories, no matter how small, and learn from any setbacks.

6. Adjust and Adapt: As you progress towards your goals, be open to adjusting your action plan as needed. Stay flexible and be willing to adapt to changing circumstances.

7. Stay Committed: Commit to your action plan and stay consistent in taking small actions towards your goals. Remember, success is a journey, not a destination, and every step you take brings you closer to your dreams.

Pick Yourself For Success

CHAPTER 11

THE POWER OF ROUTINE

"Every action you take is a vote for the person you want to become." - James Clear

In this chapter, I want to emphasize the importance of having a routine in your life. All successful people follow routines, and understanding the significance of establishing a structured daily routine can significantly impact our journey towards success.

Let's start with the word "routine" itself, which has its roots in French, meaning "road" or "path." Quite literally, your routine is the road or path you take towards either success or failure. Our habits, or routines, shape who we are and what we achieve in life. Just like an Olympic diver goes through the same routine before each dive or how bodybuilders adhere to strict diets, our routines dictate our actions and ultimately, our outcomes.

You might think routines sound boring, but that mundaneness is often the key to success. Consistently following a routine breeds discipline and consistency, essential traits for achieving long-term goals. It's about showing up every day and putting in the work, even when it feels monotonous.

I recommend starting your day by feeding your core four: mind, heart, soul, and body. Upon waking, take a moment to express gratitude. This simple act sets a positive tone for the day ahead. I grew up hearing my mother's loud declaration, "Thank you, Lord, for another day!" and I've adopted this practice into my own routine. Starting the day with gratitude shifts your focus from tasks or problems to blessings and possibilities.

Most people have a routine of watching far too much television, myself included. I confess my love for TV, but I've learned to balance it with productive activities. For example, to prioritize writing this book, I've established a routine of writing for two to three hours after my morning routine.

My morning routine consists of expressing gratitude, hydrating my body with lemon water, meditating, exercising, and feeding my mind with motivational content. I firmly believe that how you begin your day sets the tone for the rest of it. Therefore, I aim to start my day with gratitude, peace, and learning.

I typically wake up at 4 a.m. and have developed a habit of getting up immediately. Instead of hitting the snooze button, I embrace the principle of "Get up, Get Away, Get Started!" This motto, instilled in me during my time in the United States Army, reminds me to take action and start my day with purpose, regardless of the hour.

As the Army saying goes, "We do more before 6 a.m. than most people do all day." This ethos underscores the importance of seizing the early hours to accomplish meaningful tasks and set the tone for a productive day.

While some professions may require unconventional schedules, the underlying principle remains the same: Establish a routine that aligns with your goals and priorities. Whether you're a musician performing late nights or a nine-to-five worker, crafting a consistent routine sets you on the path to success.

Power Tip

Pause for a moment and assess your situation. Is there a small domino waiting to be tipped in your life? Don't hesitate. Take action now and knock it down. Embrace the momentum it creates and let it propel you forward towards your goals.

Pick Yourself For Success

CHAPTER 12

BECOME AN MVP

"True wisdom lies in recognizing the interconnectedness of Meditation, Visualization, and Prayer as the cornerstone of personal and spiritual development." - Deepak Chopra

Have you ever thought about what it takes to be a true MVP, or 'Most Valuable Player,' in life? While many associate MVP with sports, I believe that the real MVPs are those who recognize the importance of incorporating some form of Meditation, Visualization, and Prayer into their daily routines. These practices are not just reserved for spiritual gurus; they are the secret weapons of the most successful individuals among us. In this chapter, we'll explore how embracing

Meditation, Visualization, and Prayer can elevate your life to MVP status.

MEDITATION

Meditation, the M in our MVP system, serves as a cornerstone of inner peace and mindfulness. There are various ways to practice meditation, and one method I personally use is through the Fitness+ app on my iPhone. Apple offers a diverse range of guided meditations, including themes like renew, connect, and grow, with subcategories such as calm, focus, gratitude, kindness, creativity, and wisdom. Meditation comes in many forms, including mindfulness meditation, loving-kindness meditation, and transcendental meditation. It's important to note that meditation is not unique to any one spiritual practice. In fact, the Bible itself encourages meditation in Joshua 1:8 and Psalm 1:2-3, highlighting its significance in personal growth and spiritual development.

Meditation, the first component of the MVP trio, encompasses a rich tapestry of practices, each offering unique benefits for our mental, emotional, and spiritual well-being. Here are some of the most widely practiced forms of meditation.

Mindfulness Meditation

Mindfulness meditation involves focusing your attention on the present moment, observing thoughts, sensations, and emotions without judgment. It cultivates awareness and acceptance of the present reality, fostering a sense of calm and equanimity amidst life's challenges.

Loving-Kindness Meditation (Metta)

Loving-kindness meditation involves directing compassionate intentions towards oneself and others. Through the repetition of phrases like "May I be happy, may I be healthy, may I be at peace," practitioners cultivate feelings of love, empathy, and goodwill towards all beings.

Transcendental Meditation (TM)

Transcendental meditation is a technique where practitioners repeat a mantra silently, allowing the mind to transcend conscious thought and access deeper states of consciousness. It promotes relaxation, stress reduction, and increased clarity of mind.

Body Scan Meditation

Body scan meditation involves systematically scanning the body from head to toe, paying attention to physical sensations and areas of tension or discomfort. It promotes relaxation, body awareness, and stress relief by releasing physical tension and promoting a sense of ease. I usually start my sessions with a body scan.

Breath Awareness Meditation

Breath awareness meditation focuses on observing the breath as it naturally flows in and out of the body. By anchoring attention to the breath, practitioners cultivate mindfulness, concentration, and inner calm. Personally, during my practice, I've observed a unique sensation: a sense of expansion not only during inhalation. It's as if with each inhale, I'm taking up more space in the universe, deepening my connection to the present moment and enriching my meditation experience.

Visualization Meditation

Visualization meditation involves creating vivid mental images of desired outcomes or experiences. By visualizing positive scenarios, such as achieving goals, overcoming obstacles, or embodying qualities like confidence and resilience, practitioners harness the power of imagination to manifest their dreams into reality.

Mantra Meditation

Mantra meditation involves repeating a sacred word, phrase, or sound (mantra) silently or aloud. The repetition of the mantra helps quiet the mind, deepen concentration, and evoke a sense of peace and inner stillness.

These are just a few examples of the diverse range of meditation practices available. Each method offers its own unique benefits, and individuals may find that certain practices resonate more deeply with them than others. The key is to explore different techniques and find the ones that best suit your preferences and goals. Whether you're seeking relaxation, stress relief, greater self-awareness, or spiritual growth, meditation offers a powerful pathway to inner peace and personal transformation.

Visualization

Visualization, our next MVP component, is a powerful tool for manifesting our desires and creating a compelling vision for our future. Through visualization, we can align our thoughts, beliefs, and actions with our desired outcomes and attract positive opportunities into our lives. I once kept a picture of a high-end kitchen on my iPhone as a visual reminder of our aspirations for the new home we wanted. Today, I'm proud to say that we have a kitchen similar to the one I visualized, although not the exact kitchen. Through consistent visualization, we can cultivate clarity and confidence in our goals and pave the way for their manifestation.

I believe visualization is a potent tool for shaping our thoughts, beliefs, and behaviors to align with our deepest desires and aspirations. When Dr. King said "But it really doesn't matter with me now, because I've been to the mountaintop…I've seen the promised land", I believe he was describing an actual vision. So let's explore how visualization works and how we can harness its transformative power in our lives:

The Power of Mental Imagery

Visualization taps into the power of mental imagery to create vivid, detailed representations of our desired outcomes. When we visualize ourselves achieving our goals, whether it's landing a dream job, excelling in a performance, or living in our ideal home, we activate the same neural pathways in the brain as we would if we were actually experiencing those events. This primes our minds and bodies for success, making it more likely that we'll take the necessary actions to turn our visions into reality.

Creating a Compelling Vision

To harness the full potential of visualization, it's essential to create a clear and compelling vision of what we want to achieve. This involves using all of our senses to immerse ourselves in the experience, imagining the sights, sounds, smells, tastes, and feelings associated with our desired outcomes. The more vivid and detailed our mental images, the more potent their impact on our subconscious minds.

Overcoming Limiting Beliefs

Visualization is a powerful tool for overcoming limiting beliefs and self-doubt that may be holding us back from realizing our full potential. By repeatedly visualizing ourselves succeeding, we gradually reprogram our subconscious minds to believe in our abilities and possibilities. This shift in mindset empowers us to break free from self-imposed limitations and pursue our goals with confidence and conviction.

Practicing Consistently

Like any skill, visualization requires consistent practice to yield significant results. Incorporating visualization into our daily routine, whether it's through guided visualization exercises, vision boards, or mental rehearsals, strengthens our mental muscles and reinforces our commitment to our goals. The more consistently we visualize our desired outcomes, the more deeply ingrained they become in our subconscious minds, making them feel more attainable and achievable.

Celebrating Success

Visualization isn't just about imagining future success; it's also about celebrating our accomplishments along the way. Taking time to visualize and savor our achievements, no matter how small, reinforces our sense of progress and momentum, fueling our motivation to continue striving towards our goals.

Staying Flexible and Open

While visualization is a powerful tool for manifesting our desires, it's essential to remain flexible and open to unexpected opportunities and outcomes. Sometimes, God has plans for us that are even better than what we could have imagined. By maintaining a positive and open-minded attitude, we invite serendipity and synchronicity into our lives, allowing our dreams to unfold in ways we never thought possible.

By harnessing the transformative power of visualization, we can create a clear and compelling vision for our future, overcome self-limiting beliefs, and manifest our dreams with confidence and conviction. Whether we're seeking success in our careers, relationships, health, or personal growth, visualization offers a powerful pathway to realizing our full potential and living our best lives.

Prayer

Now, let's turn our attention to prayer, the final component of MVP. Prayer is a deeply personal and spiritual practice that allows us to connect with a higher power or source of guidance. Prayer doesn't have to be confined to formal rituals or kneeling in worship. We can and should pray at any time, in any place. I often take prayer walks as a way to commune with God and express my desires and intentions.

Rodney Goldston

Many years ago, when my wife and I were living in our first home, we decided we wanted to move to a more desirable neighborhood. Every morning, I would drive 25 minutes to a well-to-do neighborhood where we aspired to live, and I would walk and pray. Through these prayer walks, I made my desires known to God, and over time, our prayers were answered, and we were able to move to that neighborhood. In fact, I did it so often that people in the neighborhood mistook me for a resident. One morning, as I walked down the street, an older gentleman greeted me with a cheerful "Howdy neighbor!" I yelled "Howdy" right back at him. I took it as further confirmation of the power of consistency and faith in prayer.

I think many people pray all wrong. They pray for things. Lord give me a house, Lord please bless me with a new car. Lord please help this person to stop getting on my last nerve, yada, yada, yada. In discussing prayer, it's essential to understand that it's not just about asking for material things. Instead of praying for specific possessions or outcomes, we should pray to become the person who can achieve those desires. For instance, if you desire a brand new Mercedes Maybach, don't pray for the car itself. Instead, pray for the qualities and capabilities that would enable you to acquire such a vehicle. Pray to become the person who can do the things necessary to achieve your goals, who can buy the things you desire.

And what's the number one thing you need to pray for in order to become the person who can do the thing that can buy the thing? Wisdom. Scripture tells us that Solomon (the wisest, and wealthiest person in the Bible) didn't ask God for riches. He asked for wisdom, and because he asked for wisdom he gained wealth.

Remember, meditation, visualization, and prayer are integral components of your spiritual and personal development journey. By incorporating these practices into your daily routine, you can cultivate a deeper sense of connection, purpose, and fulfillment, and manifest your dreams with clarity and confidence. So, I encourage you to embrace these practices wholeheartedly and experience the transformative power of MVP in your life.

Power Tip

Prioritize Daily Prayer for Wisdom

Of all the things discussed here, if you only had time to do one, I suggest you pray for wisdom. If you find yourself pondering where to begin or which practice to prioritize, let wisdom be your guiding light. Dedicate time each day to prayer, seeking divine wisdom and guidance. As you cultivate wisdom within yourself, you'll discover that all other blessings naturally flow from its abundance.

Remember, wisdom isn't just about making wise decisions; it's about embodying the qualities and virtues that align with your highest self. With wisdom as your cornerstone, every step you take becomes purposeful, and every endeavor is guided by clarity and insight.

So, as you embark on your journey of personal and spiritual growth, make daily prayer for wisdom a non-negotiable part of your routine. Trust in its transformative power, and watch as it unlocks the doors to boundless possibilities and fulfillment.

Pick Yourself For Success

CHAPTER 13

GET YOUR BEAUTY REST

"Sleep is the best meditation." - The Dalai Lama

In the pursuit of greatness, it's easy to overlook the importance of deep rest. Yet, sleep plays a crucial role in our energy levels, cognitive function, and overall well-being. According to health experts, most adults require between seven to nine hours of sleep each night to function optimally. However, factors like lifestyle and individual differences can influence our sleep needs.

Pick Yourself For Success

About two decades ago, I discovered firsthand the detrimental effects of sleep deprivation. Despite rising early each morning, I failed to prioritize sufficient sleep, leading to chronic exhaustion. I vividly recall a frightening incident where I dozed off at the wheel at a stop light, narrowly avoiding a serious accident. This wakeup call prompted me to start putting my car in park at stop lights, reevaluate my sleep habits, and prioritize rest as a non-negotiable aspect of my daily routine.

One valuable lesson I learned during this time was the significance of naps. Even amidst a busy schedule, I made it a point to incorporate regular naps into my day. Whether at home or in my car during breaks, these short respites provided much-needed rejuvenation and mental clarity. Napping, I realized, was not a luxury but a necessity, especially for those not getting adequate nightly sleep.

My nap routine typically begins around 1 pm, where I prepare myself for rest just as I would for bedtime. I put on my pajamas, slip on an eye mask, and settle in for a nap lasting between 1 to 2 hours. Remarkably, even with a full night's sleep and a midday nap, I find myself naturally ready for bed by 9:00 or 10:00 pm.

The benefits of napping are supported by scientific research, as highlighted in the book "Take a Nap! Change Your Life" by Mark Ehrman and Sara C. Mednick, PhD. This powerful practice not only enhances alertness and creativity but also reduces stress, improves decision-making, and bolsters memory. Here are some tips from the book to maximize the effectiveness of your naps:

1. **Keep it Short:** Aim for a nap duration of around 20 to 30 minutes to avoid entering deep sleep stages, which can lead to grogginess upon waking.

2. **Find a Quiet Space:** Create a conducive environment for napping by minimizing noise and distractions.

3. **Stay Consistent:** Establish a regular nap schedule to reap the full benefits of this rejuvenating practice.

4. **Listen to Your Body:** Pay attention to your body's signals and allow yourself to nap when feeling fatigued or mentally drained.

Incorporating regular naps into your daily routine can be a game-changer, offering a multitude of benefits for both mind and body. By prioritizing deep rest, you'll not only enhance your performance but also elevate your overall quality of life.

Moreover, history is filled with examples of successful individuals who embraced the practice of napping. Visionaries like Winston Churchill and Salvador Dalí were known for their midday siestas, recognizing the restorative power of a brief nap. Even in today's fast-paced world, leaders like John F. Kennedy and Albert Einstein prioritized rest, acknowledging its crucial role in maintaining optimal productivity and well-being.

Pick Yourself For Success

Remember, prioritizing deep rest is not merely a luxury, but a necessity for optimal performance and well-being. Whether through nightly sleep or strategic napping, investing in quality rest is an investment in your success and vitality.

Power Tip

Think about your sleep habits, turn off digital devices after 8:00 pm so melatonin is at its best, wear an eye mask, sleep in a cool room, if you can, take a nice hot bath with epsom salts before you sleep, then take a cold shower to get more melatonin.

SECTION THREE

STEPPING INTO YOUR GREATNESS

CHAPTER 14

Follow The Light

"Stories are the light, the guide, the shelter. They carry the accumulated wisdom of our ancestors."

Have you ever felt lost in the fog? Uncertain of which direction to take? Life can be a challenging journey, and sometimes we all find ourselves wandering in the shadows, unsure of the next step. In these moments, it's crucial to remember the power of light. Light, both literal and metaphorical, serves as a beacon, guiding us out of darkness and towards a clearer path.

This chapter focuses on the illuminating power of stories. Books and documentaries can be powerful sources of inspiration, offering insights, wisdom, and even roadmaps for success. By immersing ourselves in the stories of others, we can gain valuable knowledge, discover new possibilities, and ignite a spark within ourselves.

THE POWER OF ENTERTAINMENT AND EDUCATION:

I once heard a speaker declare that watching television is a complete waste of time. While I understand the sentiment of prioritizing focused learning, I respectfully disagree. Television, like any medium, can be a powerful tool for both entertainment and education.

Let me share a personal anecdote. Growing up, television played a significant role in my world. Back then, our options were limited to the three main broadcast stations: ABC, NBC, and CBS. Each night, these channels offered a diverse range of programming, from quirky sitcoms to captivating documentaries. Shows like Star Trek, Batman, Lost in Space, and even the Jackson 5 cartoon (yes, it was a thing!) sparked my imagination, introduced me to new concepts, and fueled a lifelong love of storytelling.

The Art of Balance:

Fast forward to today, and while I still enjoy well-crafted, old school television, I recognize the importance of striking a balance between entertainment and education. My wife, a documentary enthusiast, reminds me of this every movie night! While The Terminator holds a special place in my heart, her documentary selections often surprise and inspire me.

Documentaries: A Gateway to Inspiration

Documentaries have opened my eyes to extraordinary stories of human achievement, groundbreaking scientific discoveries, and social movements that shaped our world. They offer a unique blend of education and storytelling, making complex topics engaging and accessible. Witnessing the struggles and triumphs of others can be incredibly inspiring, igniting a spark within ourselves to pursue our own goals.

Finding Inspiration on Your Screen

Today, the landscape of entertainment has exploded. Gone are the days of just three channels. Now, with the rise of cable television, streaming services, YouTube, and social media platforms, there are literally thousands of options for viewing. This vast library of content can be a powerful tool, but it's important to be mindful of how you use it.

Finding Inspiration, Avoiding Distraction

The key to using your screens as a tool for growth is to be intentional. Don't get sucked into a mindless scroll through social media feeds. Instead, leverage the power of documentaries, educational channels, and online courses to expand your knowledge and ignite your passions.

My Journey with Einstein: A Case Study

Albert Einstein is one of those figures whose story continues to inspire me. His curiosity, dedication, and groundbreaking theories about space, time, and gravity have captivated me for years. I even keep a copy of his book on the Theory of Relativity close by, a reminder of his genius and the power of intellectual exploration.

My fascination with Einstein's work didn't stop there. It led me down a path of wanting to understand the bigger picture. This journey took me deeper into the world of physics, forcing me to confront challenging concepts and expand my knowledge base. It was this pursuit that even led me to take an Intro to Physics course online at MIT. Greene's books on string theory and the nature of the universe offered a whole new perspective on reality, further fueling my thirst for knowledge.

Why Deep Dives Matter

While skimming a biography or watching a short documentary can be informative, a deep dive offers a richer and more impactful experience. Here's are some reasons why.

Unveiling the Nuances

Deep dives allow you to understand the complexities of a person's journey, including their struggles, setbacks, and ultimately, their triumphs. This comprehensive understanding is far more inspiring than a simplified narrative.

Gleaning Lessons from Mistakes

Successful people often learn valuable lessons from their failures. By delving deeper, you can identify the challenges they faced and the strategies they used to overcome them.

Identifying Common Ground

As you learn more about a person's motivations, values, and thought processes, you may discover unexpected similarities with your own. This realization can be incredibly empowering and provide a sense of connection.

Five Action Steps to Embrace Light Through Stories

1. Identify Your Inspiration:

Who are the historical figures, entrepreneurs, athletes, or artists whose stories resonate with you? Pick someone whose journey aligns with your own goals or aspirations.

2. Choose Your Materials

Explore biographies, autobiographies, documentaries, or even podcasts dedicated to your chosen figure.

3. Deep Dive

Commit to a dedicated period (a month, two months) where you immerse yourself in these resources. Take notes, underline passages that resonate with you, and actively engage with the material.

4. Identify Takeaways

After your deep dive, reflect on the key lessons you learned. How does this person's story inspire you? What specific strategies can you adapt to your own journey?

5. Take Action

Don't let inspiration remain dormant. Use the insights you gained to set new goals, overcome challenges, or ignite a new passion within yourself.

Power Tip

Focus on building a knowledge libray. Build your own personal library of inspiring stories. Fill it with books, documentaries, images, and podcasts that ignite your passions and illuminate your path to success.

Pick Yourself For Success

CHAPTER 15

SHINE YOUR LIGHT

"And God said, 'Let there be light,' and there was light." - Genesis 1:3

This powerful quote from Genesis sets the stage for our exploration of a concept as fundamental as light itself. We ended the "Stepping Out of Your Head" section with a chapter titled "Follow the Light." There, you learned that immersing yourself in the stories of those who have made significant contributions to humanity can help you escape the confines of your own thoughts. But after following the light of others, it's time to ignite your own inner flame.

We all understand light on a physical level. It illuminates our surroundings, allowing us to navigate the world around us. But light also carries a deeper meaning, a metaphorical significance. Unlike creatures with exceptional night vision, humans are particularly reliant on light. We crave it, both physically and metaphorically.

Metaphorical light represents knowledge, understanding, and inspiration. It illuminates the path ahead, guiding us through life's challenges and propelling us towards our goals. When we let our own light shine, we share that knowledge and inspiration with others, creating a ripple effect that can positively impact the world around us.

Light: A Beacon Beyond Sight

The Book of Genesis tells us that God said, "Let there be light," and there was light. What's mind blowing is that there was light in verse 3, but the sun, moon, and stars weren't created until verse 16. This powerful image reminds us that the potential for knowledge, understanding, and positive change exists within all of us, even before established structures are in place. Light represents more than physical sight; it signifies the spark of possibility, the illumination of new ideas, and the power to dispel darkness in its many forms..

John 1:5 (NKJV) tells us, "And the light shines in the darkness, and the darkness did not comprehend it." In this verse, "comprehend" doesn't necessarily mean see the light, but rather understand the significance of the light. The light represents truth, knowledge, and goodness, which can be difficult to grasp in times of darkness and confusion.

Choosing to Shine

Choosing to let your inner light shine is a powerful act. Imagine someone lost in darkness, unsure of their path. You offer an explanation, and they exclaim, "It's like a light went on inside my head!" Suddenly, their vision clears. They gain a new understanding, not just physically, but metaphorically. Your light has helped them navigate their own path.

Darkness Takes Many Forms

The darkness we face can take many shapes. It can be the darkness of ignorance, the fear that paralyzes us, or the negativity that clouds our judgment. Doubt, confusion, and a lack of knowledge can all create a sense of being lost in the dark. But by choosing to shine your light, you help others navigate these dark spaces and find their own way.

Andrew Carnegie: A Shining Example

History remembers luminous figures who illuminate the path for generations. Among them stands Andrew Carnegie. His brilliance extended beyond business and philanthropy; he actively shone his light on the darkness of societal inequality.

Carnegie's legacy is complex. He amassed wealth during industrial upheaval, yet his libraries became beacons of knowledge, offering light to those seeking education and understanding. He defied social norms by supporting Historically Black Colleges and Universities (HBCUs) at a time of racial prejudice.

Despite criticism, Carnegie believed education should be accessible to all. His support for HBCUs embodies the power of using your influence to break down barriers and empower others. True radiance comes from using your knowledge, resources, or talents to create positive change in the world.

Power Tip

Become a Beacon of Everyday Brilliance: Don't wait for a grand gesture to illuminate the world. Shine your light through everyday acts of kindness, encouragement, or knowledge sharing. A listening ear, a helping hand, or a thoughtful word can all make a big difference in someone's day.

CHAPTER 16

SERVING YOUR WAY TO SUCCESS

"You can have anything you want in life, if you help enough people get what they want in life." - Zig Ziglar

Have you ever heard the saying, "What goes around, comes around"? Well, when it comes to success, it's often true! Let's talk about the power of service and how it can lead you to your dreams.

The famous sales training coach, Zig Ziglar, taught that if you really want to be successful, you should focus on helping others first. Instead of just

Pick Yourself For Success

thinking about what you want for yourself, think about how you can use your talents and gifts to help other people. That's the secret to true success!

So, how can you figure out how to best serve others? It's simple. Just ask yourself some questions. What are you really good at? What do you enjoy doing? How can you use these skills and passions to make someone else's life better?

Think about it—some of the most successful companies and people got to where they are because they cared about making a difference. Take Home Depot, for example. They wanted to make it easy for people to fix up their homes. And Bill Gates? He wanted to make computers accessible to everyone. By focusing on their core vision and helping others, they became extremely successful.

Now, here's something important to remember: don't let anyone convince you that there's a quick and easy way to success. Those "get rich quick" schemes are trying to trick you into thinking that success comes from something outside of yourself. But guess what? True success comes from hard work and dedication.

Thomas Jefferson once said, "I'm a great believer in luck, and I find the harder I work, the more I have of it." That means, the more effort you put in, the luckier you'll get!

Sure, some people seem to find success overnight. But if you look closer, you'll see that they've probably been working at it for years. Even young athletes who make it to the Olympics started training when they were little and practiced every single day.

So, the next time you see an ad promising a quick fix for success, remember this: the real key to success is finding a way to help others. When you focus on serving people, solving their problems, and stick with it for a long time, that's when you'll find true success. So go out there and pick yourself to make a difference!

And as you embark on your journey to success, remember that my mission is to inspire others to do the things that inspire them. This book is one of the ways I'm seeking to fulfill that mission. Through corporate and personal speaking engagements, as well as coaching sessions, I aim to walk in my purpose and guide others toward their own paths of fulfillment. Remember, one of the most important keys to success is to find a problem that you can solve, one that lots of people have, and serve them by helping them to solve it. So, go forth, pick yourself, and make a difference in the world!

Power Tip

Start by asking this simple question to everyone you meet. "How can I serve you?"

Pick Yourself For Success

CHAPTER 17

BE UNCOMMON

In a world filled with common people, uncommon people are the gems that shine the brightest. - Rodney Goldston

I want to spend some time now talking with you about the concept of being uncommon. About the importance of uncommon ideas and their significance in fostering leadership and innovation, it's essential to reflect on a powerful sentiment that encapsulates the essence of this chapter. There's a quote that has always resonated deeply with me, and it fits this theme, though its attribution is uncertain. "I do not choose to be a common man. It is my right to be uncommon — if I can." While often

Pick Yourself For Success

attributed to figures like Theodore Roosevelt or Thomas Paine, its exact origins remain unclear. Regardless of its author, this quote embodies a spirit of individuality, ambition, and the pursuit of excellence that underpins the exploration of uncommon ideas.

Uncommon ideas are those that challenge the status quo, defy convention, and push the boundaries of what's possible. They are the seeds of innovation, the catalysts for change, and the fuel for progress. Embracing uncommon ideas requires courage, creativity, and a willingness to depart from the beaten path. It's about rejecting complacency and embracing the pursuit of greatness, even in the face of uncertainty and adversity.

Uncommon is not something that comes in a bottle

Uncommon is a Soul On Ice yet all out full throttle

Uncommon is Sir Nose D'Voidoffunk, and Bitches Brew

Uncommon is Marley, Parks, and Maya Angelou

Common is havin' sight but can't visualize yo' debut

Uncommon is O and Queen B

Uncommon is buying mom's a house

Uncommon is a clean mouth

Uncommon is Ali's jab

Uncommon is substance not fab

Uncommon is style and finesse

Rodney Goldston

Uncommon is flashing that S on yo' ches'

Common is sittn' court side with the team

Uncommon is owning the court and charging 'em all a fee

Common is a hive mind

Uncommon are ties that bind, might be The Fire Next Time

Uncommon is truth over lies

Uncommon is eyez on the prize

Common is doing what them fools do

Uncommon is loving yourself till every-1 else does 2

The poem you just read is my humble attempt to capture and celebrate the essence of uncommonness - that audacious spirit that has allowed generations of Black artists, leaders, and trailblazers to give a resounding voice to our humanity, our struggles, and our triumphs. From the unapologetic genius of musical pioneers like Bob Marley, George Clinton, and Miles Davis, to the piercing intellectual truth-telling of Maya Angelou, James Baldwin, and Eldridge Cleaver, to the groundbreaking cultural impact of Gordon Parks and iconic acts of resistance by Rosa Parks - this work gently nods to those uncommon ancestors and contemporaries who dared to defy oppressive conventions. When I invoke "Ali's jab", I refer not just to his unmatched physical boxing skills, but to his full identity as poetry in motion - his verbal jabs and legal stances that challenged society's injustices with uncommon valor and grace. Their bold artistry and dignity shined light on the depths of the Black experience. My aim is for this piece to ignite that same uncommon fire within us all.

Next I want to arm you with a few uncommon ideas — unique projects and initiatives that beckon for leadership. These ideas are not merely unconventional; they are bold, audacious, and ripe with potential. They offer opportunities for you to make a mark, your own ding in the universe, to carve your own path, and leave a lasting legacy.

I challenge you to embrace the call to be uncommon, to challenge the status quo, push boundaries, and create a positive impact on the world. For it is in the pursuit of uncommon ideas that you will discover your true potential and shape the future.

Power Tip

Every day, find inspiration from something uncommon. Read a poem in a strange form, listen to music from a new culture, or watch a documentary about an unusual topic.

CHAPTER 18

Uncommon People

"Be a light, not a judge. Be a model, not a critic." - Stephen Covey

In our journey towards personal growth and self-discovery, it's often illuminating to draw inspiration from those who have left an indelible mark on the world through their uncommon actions and accomplishments. In this section, I invite you to explore the lives of individuals who embody the essence of uniqueness and innovation—individuals whose mere presence reshaped the landscape of their respective fields and left an enduring legacy for generations to come.

Pick Yourself For Success

The criteria I used for selecting these uncommon individuals are guided by a simple yet profound principle: before them, nothing was quite like them, and after them, everything bore their mark. I've categorized them based on the intelligence categories of Howard Gardner's work.

These are the trailblazers, the visionaries, and the innovators whose unwavering commitment to their passions and unyielding determination propelled them to greatness. Their stories serve as powerful reminders of the boundless potential that lies within each of us and the transformative impact we can have when we dare to embrace our uniqueness and pursue our dreams with fervor.

As we journey through the lives of these uncommon individuals, you'll witness the diverse manifestations of human potential across different realms of intelligence, creativity, and innovation. From groundbreaking inventors and pioneering scientists to visionary artists and influential leaders, each individual selected for examination offers a distinct perspective on what it means to defy convention, challenge the status quo, and leave an indelible imprint on the world.

By exploring the uncommon achievements of these extraordinary individuals, you'll glean valuable insights into the power of courage, resilience, and unwavering dedication in the pursuit of greatness. Their stories serve as beacons of inspiration, guiding you on your own quest for personal growth, fulfillment, and meaningful contribution to the world.

Join me as we embark on a journey of discovery, exploration, and inspiration, guided by the lives and legacies of uncommon people and the uncommon things they've done. Together, let's celebrate the transformative power of human potential and the boundless possibilities that await those who dare to dream boldly and act courageously.

LINGUISTIC INTELLIGENCE

This intelligence involves the ability to effectively use language to communicate, write, and understand spoken and written words. People strong in this area excel in reading, writing, storytelling, and public speaking.

MARTIN LUTHER KING JR.: THE VOICE OF A MOVEMENT

There's a strong case to be made that Dr. Martin Luther King Jr., a Baptist minister from Atlanta, Georgia, deserves a place among the greatest Americans, possibly even one of the most influential figures in human history. His exceptional Linguistic Intelligence wasn't just about oratory; it was about using words to stir conscience, ignite a movement, and forever alter the course of history. Dr. King's message of hope and love, delivered with unparalleled eloquence, resonated far beyond the shores of the United States, inspiring people around the world.

Before Dr. King

The fight for racial equality relied on traditional methods like protests and legal challenges. Public discourse on the issue was often limited and lacked the power to capture the hearts and minds of a nation.

After Dr. King

Dr. King's arrival on the scene marked a turning point. His powerful speeches, infused with biblical allusions, metaphors, and soaring cadences, transcended race and resonated with millions. He didn't just speak about equality; he painted a picture of a future brimming with justice and opportunity for all.

The Power of Words

Dr. King's Linguistic Intelligence manifested in several ways:

Masterful Rhetoric: His speeches were meticulously crafted, using rhetorical devices like repetition, parallelism, and powerful imagery to create a lasting impact. Consider the iconic "I Have a Dream" speech, where King's repeated refrain of "Let freedom ring" became a rallying cry for a nation.

Emotional Connection: Dr. King understood the power of language to evoke emotions. He used metaphors and similes to paint vivid pictures of injustice and the yearning for freedom. His words resonated with the hopes and aspirations of millions, uniting them in the cause for civil rights.

Beyond Oratory:

Dr. King's linguistic intelligence wasn't confined to public speeches. His writings, including his famous "Letter from Birmingham Jail," eloquently argued for the moral imperative of civil disobedience. He understood the importance of clear and concise communication in galvanizing a movement.

A Legacy of Change:

Dr. Martin Luther King Jr.'s legacy extends far beyond the words he spoke. His exceptional Linguistic Intelligence empowered a generation, inspiring peaceful protest and dismantling racial barriers. He showed the world the transformative power of language, using it as a weapon of justice and a bridge towards a more equitable future. His message of hope and love continues to inspire people around the world, making him a true global icon.

William Shakespeare: The Bard of Avon and Master of Language

Imagine a time before elaborate sets and special effects dominated the theater. Enter William Shakespeare, a playwright from England, who wielded language with such mastery that it transported audiences and redefined dramatic storytelling. Shakespeare's exceptional Linguistic Intelligence wasn't just about vocabulary; it was about using words to paint vivid pictures, evoke emotions, and create characters that have resonated for centuries.

Before Shakespeare:

Theater consisted of established forms with limited emotional depth and character development. Language played a functional role, but lacked the power to truly captivate audiences.

After Shakespeare:

Shakespeare's arrival on the scene revolutionized theater. He infused his plays with rich imagery, invented new words, and crafted dialogue that delivered humor, pathos, and profound truths about the human condition. His characters, from the star-crossed lovers Romeo and Juliet to the power-hungry Macbeth, transcended the stage and became timeless archetypes.

THE POWER OF WORDS:

Shakespeare's Linguistic Intelligence manifested in several ways:

Mastery of Vocabulary: Shakespeare possessed an unparalleled vocabulary, using language in a way that was both rich and accessible. He even invented hundreds of words that are still used today, demonstrating his ability to shape the very fabric of the English language.

Vivid Imagery: Shakespeare's words weren't just sounds; they were brushstrokes painting vivid pictures in the minds of the audience. His metaphors, similes, and evocative descriptions transported audiences to different worlds and allowed them to experience the emotions of his characters firsthand.

Unforgettable Characters: Shakespeare's characters are some of the most enduring in all of literature. He brought them to life through their language, allowing audiences to connect with their desires, flaws, and profound humanity.

A Legacy that Inspires:

William Shakespeare's legacy extends far beyond the Elizabethan era. His exceptional Linguistic Intelligence transformed theater, enriched the English language, and continues to inspire actors, writers, and audiences around the world. He didn't just write plays; he provided a wellspring of themes, characters, and storytelling techniques that continue to influence modern cinema. From the epic scope of historical dramas to the poignant emotions of romantic comedies, Shakespeare's influence can be felt across a wide range of genres. His mastery of language allows his stories to transcend time and culture, making him a true titan of the theater.

A Bard Encounter:

Like countless others, I was introduced to the magic of Shakespeare in high school. My English teacher, Mrs. Cavenaugh (a true champion of the Bard!), had us delve into several of his plays, including the iconic Romeo and Juliet and the chilling Macbeth. To solidify our understanding, part of our final grade hinged on reciting lines from these plays. Confession time: I vividly remember showing up to class that day, emboldened by the promise of extra credit, sporting a pair of tights (don't ask!) and enthusiastically delivering the unforgettable lines, "Tomorrow, and tomorrow, and tomorrow, creeps in this petty pace from day to day." While the memory of the tights might fade, the impact of Shakespeare's words and Mrs. Cavenaugh's passion for literature has remained with me ever since.

Toni Morrison: A Literary Griot

A Nobel Prize-winning novelist who redefined American literature with her powerful exploration of race, identity, and the African American experience.

Before Toni Morrison:

American literature, while rich and diverse, hadn't fully explored the complexities of the Black American experience, particularly from a Black woman's perspective.

Themes of race, slavery, and the psychological impact of oppression were often absent or presented through a white lens.

After Toni Morrison:

Morrison revolutionized American literature by centering the Black experience in her powerful novels. She gave voice to characters and stories previously marginalized.

Her exploration of race, identity, and the legacy of slavery forever changed the literary landscape, influencing generations of writers.

HERE ARE SOME SPECIFIC EXAMPLES OF HOW TONI MORRISON LEFT HER MARK:

Pioneering voice

Her novels, like "Beloved" and "The Bluest Eye," broke new ground by tackling sensitive themes from a Black perspective, forcing readers to confront uncomfortable truths.

Shifting the narrative

She challenged the white gaze in literature, offering a nuanced and authentic portrayal of Black characters and communities.

Literary Legacy

Morrison's influence can be seen in the work of countless contemporary writers who explore race and social justice in their work.

In essence, Toni Morrison didn't just write novels; she redefined American literature. She opened doors for other Black writers and ensured that the Black experience would be a central voice in American storytelling.

MUSICAL INTELLIGENCE

This intelligence involves the ability to perceive, perform, and create music. People strong in this area have a natural aptitude for music, rhythm, and melody. They may excel at playing instruments, composing music, or singing.

RICHARD WAYNE PENNIMAN

American music boasts a rich tapestry of genres, from the soulful strains of blues and gospel to the driving rhythms of rock and roll and the smooth melodies of R&B. A strong case can be made for Richard Wayne Penneyman as the most influential performer in American music history. Thus, any serious conversation about musical intelligence in this vibrant landscape deserves a central place for Richard Wayne Penniman, better known as Little Richard. Little Richard's music significantly shaped and redefined these genres, particularly Rock and Roll. His influence extends across the spectrum of American music, making him a true pioneer.

His dynamic voice and infectious personality helped define these genres, influencing countless musicians and leaving an enduring legacy.

Before Little Richard:

American popular music existed in various forms, including rhythm and blues, country, and pop. These genres were largely segregated, with distinct sounds and audiences, and rock and roll, as a unified genre, didn't exist.

After Little Richard:

Little Richard's electrifying music, with its blend of blues, gospel, and boogie-woogie, transcended racial and cultural barriers. He ushered in a new era of music – rock and roll – that united young audiences across America.

His influence can be felt not just in rock and roll, but in virtually every genre that followed. From the raw energy of punk to the soulful vocals of R&B, musicians across genres have drawn inspiration from Little Richard. A few weeks after Little Richard's death Elton John stated on his Twitter feed, now X, "He was one of my biggest influences and our duet, The Power, is one of my favorite tracks that I've ever recorded." - Elton John

Pick Yourself For Success

HERE'S WHY SOME CALL HIM THE "FATHER" OF AMERICAN MUSIC:

Bridging the Gap: He broke down racial barriers in music, bringing together black and white audiences. His music resonated with a generation yearning for a new sound.

Universal Appeal: His music transcended genre and language. The raw energy, powerful vocals, and driving rhythms resonated with a global audience hungry for something fresh and exciting.

DNA of Modern Music: The core elements of rock and roll – driving rhythms, powerful vocals, and emphasis on performance – are present in countless genres today. Little Richard's music is the foundation upon which much of modern music is built.

Little Richard wasn't just a rock and roll pioneer; he was a transformative figure in American music. His influence continues to resonate across genres and generations, making him a truly "uncommon person" who left an indelible mark on the world.

ARETHA FRANKLIN: QUEEN OF SOUL

"RESPECT find out what it means to me." I get a 'funk-face' just writing that. I'm of the opinion that some music should never be redone by another artist. In fact it's difficult for me to fathom any artist redoing an Aretha original and doing anything that could possibly make it better.

Aretha Franklin didn't just exist within the existing landscape of soul music, she fundamentally changed it. Her influence on music and popular culture is undeniable, making her a perfect example for our list of "Uncommon People."

Before Aretha:

Soul music existed, but it lacked a strong female voice with the power and emotional depth that Franklin brought.

Gospel music heavily influenced soul, but the secular world hadn't seen a vocalist like Franklin who could seamlessly blend the power and passion of gospel with the raw energy of R&B.

After Aretha:

Countless female singers were influenced by her powerful vocals, stage presence, and ability to infuse soul music with social commentary.

Artists like Tina Turner, Whitney Houston, Mariah Carey, and Alicia Keys all owe a debt to Franklin's pioneering work.

She redefined what it meant to be a female vocalist, paving the way for a new generation of powerful women in music.

Here are some specific examples of how Aretha left her mark:

Genre-bending:

She blurred the lines between gospel, R&B, and pop, creating a unique sound that resonated with a wider audience.

Social Commentary:

Songs like "Respect" and "Think" became anthems for the Civil Rights and feminist movements.

Vocal Power:

Her powerful, expressive voice set a new standard for female singers in soul and R&B.

The impact of these musical pioneers – Little Richard and Aretha Franklin – is undeniable. Their legacies continue to inspire countless musicians. Yet, the world of music boasts countless other uncommon minds. From the defiant symphonies of a deaf Beethoven to the scorching guitar solos of Jimi Hendrix, the introspective lyrics of Bob Dylan, and the electrifying performances of Michael Jackson, the landscape of music is forever altered by those who dare to push boundaries. This is just a glimpse into the vast spectrum of musical intelligence. I encourage you to delve deeper, explore these and other musical icons, and discover the stories and innovations that continue to shape the world of sound.

Visual-Spatial Intelligence

This intelligence involves the ability to perceive the world visually and spatially. People strong in this area excel in tasks like drawing, interpreting maps, visualizing objects in 3D, and navigating through space.

Gordon Parks: Bearing Witness Through Lens and Light

A trailblazing photographer, filmmaker, and writer, Parks used his visual storytelling skills to shed light on social issues and capture the beauty of everyday life. His iconic images and films challenged stereotypes and inspired social change, leaving an indelible mark on American culture.

As a photographer and filmmaker, Parks possessed a remarkable eye for composition, lighting, and capturing the essence of a scene. He used his visual-spatial intelligence to tell powerful stories through his work.

Pick Yourself For Success

Before Gordon Parks:

Photojournalism often lacked diversity in perspective and subject matter. Images typically focused on established narratives, with less emphasis on social justice issues faced by marginalized communities. Representation of African American photographers was limited.

After Gordon Parks:

Gordon Parks became a pioneering photographer who broke racial barriers in the field. He was the first African American staff photographer at Life magazine, a major leadership position.

His work redefined photojournalism by using his camera as a powerful tool for social commentary. He captured the struggles and triumphs of African Americans and the underprivileged, bringing their unseen realities to a wider audience.

His iconic photo "A Negro Jazz Musician in Harlem" (featuring musician Roy DeCarava) is considered one of the most famous jazz photos ever taken, inspiring countless imitations.

Parks' influence extended beyond photography. His groundbreaking film "Shaft," featuring a strong, complex Black protagonist, shattered stereotypes and opened doors for a generation of Black filmmakers like Spike Lee and Tyler Perry. Furthermore, "Shaft" paved the way for more Black actors to take on leading roles in Hollywood, paving the way for careers like Denzel Washington.

Gordon Parks' Visual-Spatial Intelligence:

Parks' remarkable visual-spatial intelligence was evident in his photography.

Composition:

His photos used exceptional composition, drawing viewers in with leading lines, framing, and negative space.

Lighting:

He masterfully used lighting to create mood and atmosphere, highlighting details that conveyed the emotions and realities of his subjects.

Capturing the Moment:

Parks had an uncanny ability to capture fleeting moments of human emotion and vulnerability, creating a powerful connection with the viewer.

Beyond Technique:

Parks' visual intelligence went beyond technical mastery. He possessed a keen eye for social justice, using his camera to document the struggles of the underprivileged and advocate for change. His work transcended aesthetics, becoming a powerful voice for social progress.

A Legacy of Impact:

Gordon Parks' legacy extends far beyond his groundbreaking achievements. His work continues to inspire generations of photographers, filmmakers, and activists. He redefined visual storytelling, using his visual-spatial intelligence to create a more just and equitable world.

Misty Copeland: A Ballerina for a New Era

Imagine a world of graceful movement, where the human body becomes an instrument of storytelling. Ballet, a centuries-old art form, embodies this ideal. But for many, the image of a ballerina may conjure a specific body type or ethnicity. Enter Misty Copeland, a dancer who shattered these limitations and redefined the lines of dance through her exceptional talent and unwavering dedication.

Before Misty Copeland:

Traditionally, ballet dancers have conformed to a particular aesthetic. Representation of African Americans in these prestigious companies was rare.

Rodney Goldston

A Star Is Born:

Misty Copeland's arrival on the ballet scene challenged these narrow perceptions. Her journey began far from the grand stages of renowned ballet companies. With limited resources and facing societal expectations, she discovered ballet at a young age and poured her heart into the art form. Years of relentless practice honed her skills, and her natural talent for dance began to shine.

Breaking Barriers:

Copeland's exceptional visual-spatial intelligence became evident in her remarkable technique. Ballet demands a deep understanding of the body in space. Dancers must translate visual cues from choreography into precise movements, all while maintaining awareness of their surroundings to avoid collisions. Copeland excelled in this area, interpreting complex choreography with grace and fluidity.

Beyond Technique: A Visual Storyteller

But Copeland's brilliance extends beyond technical prowess. She possesses a keen visual sense, evident in her ability to interpret and embody the emotions and narratives conveyed through ballet. Her performances transcend mere steps; they become stories told through movement.

A Legacy of Inspiration:

Misty Copeland's groundbreaking achievement as the first African American principal ballerina at the prestigious American Ballet Theatre (ABT) transcended the world of dance. Her story resonated with a wider audience, inspiring young dancers of all backgrounds to pursue their dreams in ballet. She not only redefined who could excel in this demanding art form, but also opened doors for a more inclusive future.

Misty Copeland's journey is an inspiring example of visual-spatial intelligence in action. It's a testament to the power of dedication, perseverance, and the ability to translate vision into reality.

Pablo Picasso: The Untamed Bull of Art - A Force of Nature Who Changed the Course of Art History

Imagine a world where art followed a rigid rulebook. Paintings presented objects and people in a single, unchanging way, focused on replicating reality exactly as the eye saw it. This was the art world before Pablo Picasso, a Spanish artist whose exceptional visual-spatial intelligence would forever alter the way we perceive the world.

Before Picasso:

Traditionally, art adhered to established forms of representation. Paintings focused on realism, depicting the world with a single, fixed perspective.

After Picasso:

Picasso shattered these conventions. His groundbreaking style, Cubism, fragmented objects and figures, reassembling them from multiple perspectives on a single canvas. This challenged viewers' perception of space and form, asking them to question how they see the world. His work shattered the boundaries of traditional representation and ushered in a new era of artistic expression.

Picasso's Visual-Spatial Intelligence:

Picasso's exceptional visual-spatial intelligence wasn't just about technical mastery; it allowed him to see the world in extraordinary ways.

Fractured and Whole:

He could deconstruct objects and figures in his mind, then reassemble them from various viewpoints simultaneously. This is evident in his Cubist works, where a single subject is depicted from multiple perspectives on a single canvas.

Space Untamed:

Traditional rules of perspective couldn't contain his vision. Cubism challenged these limitations, yet his paintings maintained a sense of balance and coherence, showcasing his mastery of spatial composition.

Vision into Form:

Picasso's ability to translate his visual concepts into groundbreaking artistic forms demonstrates the true power of his visual-spatial intelligence.

LOGICAL-MATHEMATICAL INTELLIGENCE

This intelligence focuses on logical reasoning, problem-solving, and mathematical thinking. Individuals with high logical-mathematical intelligence excel at analyzing data, identifying patterns, and coming up with solutions through a logical approach.

HIDDEN FIGURES: THE MATHEMATICIANS WHO LAUNCHED DREAMS

Imagine a time before the whirring of computers filled the halls of NASA. Calculations for space missions were meticulously performed by hand, a process that was both laborious and prone to error. Then came the "Hidden Figures," a trio of brilliant African American women – Katherine Johnson,

Dorothy Vaughan, and Mary Jackson – who defied racial and gender barriers to make groundbreaking contributions with their exceptional logical-mathematical intelligence.

Before the Hidden Figures:

Traditionally, the world of mathematics and engineering lacked diversity. Calculations for space missions were a slow and manual endeavor, limiting the potential for innovation.

After the Hidden Figures:

The arrival of Katherine Johnson, Dorothy Vaughan, and Mary Jackson at NASA revolutionized the way the agency approached problem-solving. Johnson's expertise in analytical geometry and orbital mechanics proved invaluable. Her calculations were instrumental in the success of John Glenn's historic orbit around the Earth, ensuring his safe return. Vaughan, a mathematical whiz with a keen eye for efficiency, championed the use of IBM computers at NASA. This pioneering move significantly reduced calculation times and ushered in a new era of technological advancement at the agency. Jackson, after overcoming barriers to become NASA's first Black female engineer, applied her problem-solving skills to tackle various aerospace challenges.

Logical-Mathematical Minds at Work:

Each of these women displayed exceptional logical-mathematical intelligence.

Katherine Johnson:

Her ability to analyze complex data and perform intricate calculations related to orbital mechanics was unmatched. She could break down complex problems, identify solutions, and ensure the accuracy of flight trajectories – a skill critical for the success of space missions.

Dorothy Vaughan:

Her proficiency in mathematics went beyond calculations. Vaughan possessed a strong analytical mind and a vision for the future. She recognized the potential of computers to revolutionize the way NASA handled data, and her foresight led to a more efficient and streamlined approach.

Mary Jackson:

Jackson's engineering background equipped her with a unique blend of logical thinking and problem-solving skills. She could apply her knowledge of mathematics and physics to tackle real-world engineering challenges, a crucial asset for various aerospace projects.

BEYOND CALCULATIONS: THE POWER OF REASON

The brilliance of the "Hidden Figures" goes beyond their technical expertise. These women possessed exceptional reasoning abilities and unwavering perseverance. They could break down complex problems, identify flaws in existing systems, and persist through challenges – all hallmarks of logical-mathematical intelligence.

A Legacy of Inspiration:

The story of the "Hidden Figures" is more than a historical footnote. It's a testament to the power of logical-mathematical intelligence to push the boundaries of human achievement. These women shattered barriers, inspired generations to pursue careers in STEM fields, and proved that brilliance can come from the most unexpected places. Their legacy continues to inspire mathematicians, engineers, and dreamers of all backgrounds to reach for the stars.

EDWARD DEMING: THE ARCHITECT OF QUALITY

Ever wondered why Toyota and Honda consistently rank among the most reliable car brands in the world? The answer lies with a brilliant American statistician named W. Edwards Deming. Deming's exceptional Logical-Mathematical Intelligence revolutionized the concept of quality, and his influence is felt not just in the auto industry but across various sectors.

Imagine a world of manufacturing where products are inconsistent, and quality control is a guessing game. Enter W. Edwards Deming, who challenged this status quo with his logical mind and keen problem-solving skills. Deming's work transformed not only manufacturing but also ushered in a new era of data-driven decision making across various industries.

Before Deming:

Prior to Deming's influence, quality control often relied on intuition and guesswork. There was a lack of focus on continuous improvement, and data wasn't systematically used to identify and address problems.

After Deming:

Deming's arrival on the scene transformed how businesses approached quality. He is best known for developing the Deming cycle, also known as the Plan-Do-Check-Act (PDCA) cycle. This foundational concept involves a logical, data-driven approach to continuous improvement.

DEMING'S LOGICAL-MATHEMATICAL INTELLIGENCE AT WORK:

Statistical Expertise:

He was a master statistician, able to analyze data to identify trends, understand process variations, and pinpoint areas for improvement.

Rodney Goldston

Problem-Solving Through Data:

Deming didn't rely on hunches; he used data as the foundation for solving problems and making decisions. This focus on data-driven decision making is a hallmark of logical-mathematical intelligence.

Systems Thinking:

Deming viewed organizations as interconnected systems. He understood that quality wasn't just about individual products but about optimizing the entire production process.

Beyond Manufacturing:

Deming's impact extended far beyond the manufacturing sector. His emphasis on data-driven decision making, continuous improvement, and a focus on customer satisfaction influenced various industries, including healthcare, education, and service sectors.

A Legacy of Quality:

Edward Deming's legacy is undeniable. His logical approach to quality control, built on a foundation of data analysis and continuous improvement, transformed manufacturing practices worldwide. He showed how logical-mathematical intelligence can be harnessed to achieve excellence and create a culture of quality that benefits not just businesses but also consumers.

Interpersonal Intelligence

This intelligence focuses on understanding and interacting effectively with others. Individuals with high interpersonal intelligence are often good at reading people's emotions, building relationships, and resolving conflicts.

Richard Pryor: Revolutionizing Comedy Through Connection

Imagine a comedic landscape in the mid-20th century in which stand-up comedy was largely segregated, with Black performers facing limited opportunities. Their routines, while addressing Black experiences, rarely crossed over to mainstream audiences. Jokes on sensitive topics like race, sex, and politics were generally avoided in favor of lighter observational humor.

Film comedies also reflected this segregated reality. Black actors were often relegated to stereotypical roles, and comedic opportunities were scarce. While comedic acting legends like Charlie Chaplin might utilize costume changes, their characters remained singular within a film.

Then came Richard Pryor, a comedic force unlike any other. As Scott Saul, author of "Becoming Richard Pryor," aptly states, Pryor seemed to exist "on the very edge of the culture and, from another, seem to reorient the center of the culture around them." His genius wasn't just in his raw humor, but in his exceptional interpersonal intelligence. He possessed an uncanny ability to connect with audiences from all backgrounds, shattering racial barriers in stand-up. His routines tackled sensitive social issues head-on, using humor to spark dialogue and force audiences to confront uncomfortable truths.

Beyond Stand-Up: A Legacy of Character Innovation

Pryor's influence wasn't limited to stand-up. He was a groundbreaking comedic actor in film, pioneering the art of playing multiple characters within a single scene. His ability to seamlessly switch between characters showcased his versatility and comedic genius. This innovative approach paved the way for future comedic giants like Eddie Murphy's multiple roles in "The Nutty Professor," Mike Myers' shape-shifting characters in the "Austin Powers" franchise, the many characters played by Dave Chappelle on the Chappelle Show, and Tyler Perry's iconic Madea character.

THE INTRAPERSONAL WELLSPRING OF COMEDY

Placing Pryor neatly within Howard Gardner's system of intelligences is a challenge, because he embodied strengths from multiple areas. His interpersonal brilliance is undeniable, but his humor also stemmed from a deep well of intrapersonal intelligence. He wasn't afraid to delve into his own vulnerabilities and inner struggles, using them as a springboard to explore the broader human experience. This willingness to be painfully honest resonated with audiences, creating a unique sense of connection and intimacy.

Pryor's Interpersonal Brilliance: A Lasting Impact

Richard Pryor's story exemplifies the power of both interpersonal and intrapersonal intelligence. He wasn't afraid to be uncommon, to push boundaries, and to connect with people on a deep level through humor. His legacy continues to inspire artists and comedians who understand the power of humor to challenge, unite, and make us think critically.

Interpersonal intelligence isn't limited to the world of entertainment. Consider the transformative power of figures like Nelson Mandela, who fostered reconciliation between races in South Africa. Gandhi's unwavering commitment to non-violent resistance required a deep understanding of human connection. Mother Teresa's lifelong dedication to serving the poorest of the poor stemmed from her profound ability to connect with people in their suffering.

These individuals, along with countless others, demonstrate the transformative power of interpersonal intelligence. It allows us to build bridges, foster empathy, and create positive change in the world. Richard Pryor, the comedic genius who dared to be different, serves as a powerful reminder that this intelligence can take many forms, and its impact can be truly remarkable.

INTRAPERSONAL INTELLIGENCE

This intelligence focuses on understanding oneself and one's internal world. People strong in this area are introspective and self-aware. They excel at setting goals, understanding their motivations, and making independent decisions.

MAYA ANGELOU: A PIONEERING VOICE OF RESILIENCE, IDENTITY, AND THE #METOO MOVEMENT

Before Maya:

The landscape of American literature, particularly autobiography, often lacked a focus on the experiences of Black women. While powerful voices like Langston Hughes and Zora Neale Hurston existed, a significant gap remained in fully exploring the intersection of race, gender, and trauma. Discussions of sexual violence were particularly shrouded in silence.

The Unprecedented Voice of Maya Angelou:

Maya Angelou emerged as a literary force unlike any other. Her groundbreaking autobiography, "I Know Why the Caged Bird Sings," shattered the mold. With unflinching honesty, she delved into the complexities of growing up Black and female in a segregated America, confronting issues of sexual assault, racism, and poverty. This raw vulnerability resonated deeply with readers across racial and cultural backgrounds, paving the way for a new wave of literature that addressed previously silenced experiences.

After Maya:

The impact of Maya Angelou's work is undeniable. Here's how she changed the world:

Literary Revolution:

Angelou's success opened doors for a new generation of Black women writers to explore themes of identity, resilience, and social justice. Her influence can be seen in the works of Toni Morrison, Alice Walker, and countless others.

Shifting Cultural Landscape:

Her powerful voice in literature and activism empowered Black women to find their voice and claim their space in society.

Universal Resonance:

Beyond race, Angelou's exploration of human emotions and experiences with trauma and survival resonated with readers worldwide.

Foremother of the #Me Too Movement: By bravely recounting her experience of sexual assault, Angelou broke the long-held silence surrounding sexual violence. This act of public disclosure in 1969 anticipated a core principle of the #MeToo movement - giving voice to survivors.

A Legacy of Inspiration:

Maya Angelou's groundbreaking work didn't just fill a void; it reshaped the literary landscape. She gave voice to the silenced, empowered a generation, and forever changed the way we think about identity, resilience, and the power of the human spirit. Her courage in speaking her truth undoubtedly paved the way for the #MeToo movement and the countless survivors who found strength in her voice.

Pick Yourself for Success:

Maya Angelou's life serves as a powerful reminder that greatness often lies in embracing your unique voice and experiences. Ask yourself: What story are you waiting to tell? What challenges have shaped you into the person you are today? By sharing your truth and experiences, you can inspire others and contribute to a more inclusive and powerful world.

Following the Uncommon Path:

Maya Angelou stands as a testament to the transformative power of intrapersonal intelligence. But she's not alone. History is filled with individuals who embarked on uncommon journeys of self-discovery and used their insights to leave an indelible mark on the world. Here are a few names to consider for further exploration:

ARISTOTLE:

Widely regarded as the "father of logic," Aristotle wasn't just a brilliant thinker; he was a master of introspection. He emphasized the importance of self-examination and critical thinking in his pursuit of knowledge, laying the foundation for Western philosophy and scientific inquiry.

NELSON MANDELA:

Imprisoned for 27 years, Mandela used his solitary confinement to cultivate inner strength and forgiveness. He emerged to lead South Africa through a historic transition to democracy, demonstrating the power of self-reflection and perseverance.

LEONARDO DA VINCI:

This polymath wasn't just an artist or inventor; he was a master of self-directed learning. His in-depth anatomical studies, engineering notebooks, and artistic explorations all demonstrate a profound curiosity about the world and himself. His relentless pursuit of knowledge and self-improvement embodies intrapersonal intelligence.

Viktor Frankl:

A Holocaust survivor and psychiatrist, Frankl developed the concept of logotherapy, focusing on finding meaning in life even amidst suffering. His own experiences in concentration camps forced him to confront the depths of human existence and discover the power of the human spirit. His journey of self-discovery and his focus on inner meaning make him a strong example.

Harriet Tubman:

An escaped slave and conductor on the Underground Railroad, Tubman displayed exceptional self-awareness and courage. She relied on her own internal compass and deep understanding of human nature to navigate perilous journeys and guide others to freedom. Her focus on self-reliance and inner strength makes her a great example.

Naturalistic Intelligence

This intelligence focuses on understanding and interacting with the natural world. Individuals with high naturalistic intelligence have a strong connection to nature and are often interested in plants, animals, and the environment.

JANE GOODALL: A CHAMPION FOR NATURE WITH UNPARALLELED NATURALISTIC INTELLIGENCE

Before Jane:

The world of animal behavior research was dominated by observation from afar. Animals were often studied in captivity, leading to an incomplete understanding of their natural behaviors and social interactions.

A Pioneering Approach:

Jane Goodall, a young woman with a passion for chimpanzees, dared to be different. She revolutionized the field of primatology with her groundbreaking research conducted in Gombe Stream National Park, Tanzania. Goodall's approach embodied exceptional naturalistic intelligence.

NATURALISTIC INTELLIGENCE IN ACTION:

Keen Observation: Goodall spent years meticulously observing chimpanzees in their natural habitat. Her patience and attentiveness allowed her to document a complex social hierarchy, tool use, and even emotional expressions among the chimps, previously unseen behaviors.

Rodney Goldston

Pattern Recognition: Goodall's sharp mind excelled at identifying patterns in chimpanzee behavior. She meticulously recorded interactions, feeding habits, and communication methods, building a comprehensive understanding of their social lives.

Deep Connection with Nature: Goodall possessed an innate ability to connect with the natural world. Her respect and understanding of the chimpanzees allowed her to gain their trust, resulting in groundbreaking observations that challenged existing scientific knowledge.

Beyond Observation:

Goodall's work transcended the collection of data. Her deep empathy for chimpanzees and her understanding of their intelligence fueled her lifelong commitment to conservation.

A Legacy of Environmental Awareness:

Jane Goodall's groundbreaking research not only revolutionized our understanding of chimpanzees, but also ignited a global movement for environmental awareness. Here's how:

Bridging the Gap Between Humans and Animals: Goodall's work challenged the notion of human exceptionalism, highlighting the cognitive abilities and emotional complexity of chimpanzees. This understanding fostered a greater appreciation for all life forms.

Conservation Champion:

Goodall's advocacy for chimpanzee habitat protection and her fight against deforestation inspired a generation of conservationists. Her work serves as a powerful reminder of the interconnectedness of all living things.

Inspiring the Next Generation: Goodall's tireless dedication to environmental education has sparked a passion for nature in countless individuals. Her message of respect and responsibility for the natural world continues to inspire future generations.

THE PATH OF NATURALISTIC INTELLIGENCE:

Jane Goodall isn't alone. History is filled with individuals who have harnessed the power of naturalistic intelligence:

CHARLES DARWIN:

This naturalist's meticulous observations during his voyage on the HMS Beagle led to the groundbreaking theory of evolution by natural selection. His keen eye for detail and ability to connect seemingly disparate observations revolutionized our understanding of the natural world.

CHARLES WINICK:

This ornithologist's passion for birds led to the development of bird banding, a crucial tool for tracking bird migration patterns and population health. His detailed observations and innovative methods exemplified naturalistic intelligence.

Dian Fossey:

A primatologist dedicated to gorilla conservation, Fossey spent years studying these majestic creatures in their Rwandan habitat. Her patience, observational skills, and deep connection with the gorillas provided invaluable insights into their social behavior and threats to their survival.

These are just a few examples. The natural world holds countless wonders waiting to be discovered.

Pick Yourself for Success:

Consider ways to nurture your own naturalistic intelligence. Spend time outdoors, observe the world around you with curiosity, and appreciate the intricate dance of life in nature. Every step you take towards understanding and appreciating the natural world is a step towards a more sustainable future.

Power Tip

Pick Yourself For Success

Create a physical or digital "uncommon inspiration board" that features quotes, images, and stories of people who embody uncommon characteristics. This will serve as a daily reminder of what it means to be uncommon and inspire you to pursue your own uncommon path.

CHAPTER 19

FINDING BEAUTY IN BROKENNESS

"You think your pain and your heartbreak are unprecedented in the history of the world, but then you read. It was Dostoevsky and Dickens who taught me that the things that tormented me most were the very things that connected me with all the people who were alive, or whoever had been alive. Only if we face these open wounds in ourselves can we understand them in other people." - James Baldwin

We all experience brokenness in life, as author James Baldwin reflects, leaving us feeling lost, defeated, and even shattered. Perhaps you've experienced setbacks, loss, or hardship that left you feeling flawed and imperfect. In these moments, it's easy to feel defeated or hopeless, to believe you'll never be whole again. But what if your brokenness isn't something to hide, but an opportunity for growth?

Kintsugi, a Japanese art form, offers a powerful metaphor for embracing imperfection and finding beauty in brokenness. Unlike discarding broken pottery, Kintsugi practitioners meticulously repair the pieces using a special adhesive mixed with gold, silver, or platinum. The result? A one-of-a-kind, striking piece of art that celebrates, rather than hides, the cracks and imperfections. The broken areas are not just repaired, but enhanced, making the object stronger and more beautiful than before.

More Than Just Pottery Repair: A Metaphor for Life

Kintsugi is more than just a mending technique; it's a profound metaphor for life's journey. Just as the pottery endures challenges, so do we. The cracks and fractures represent the inevitable hardships we face. But Kintsugi offers a powerful lesson: Our brokenness is not a sign of weakness, but a testament to our resilience.

The repair process, using precious metals, symbolizes the value and beauty of imperfection. The seams of gold transform the broken pieces into something extraordinary, highlighting their unique character. Similarly, your scars and flaws can be filled with wisdom, compassion, and strength.

Through healing and growth, you emerge stronger, wiser, and more beautiful than before.

Embracing Imperfection for True Freedom

Kintsugi also reminds us that perfection is an illusion. It's the acceptance of our imperfections that leads to true freedom and authenticity. In a world obsessed with flawlessness, Kintsugi celebrates the beauty of what makes us unique. It teaches us to embrace our vulnerabilities, recognizing them as essential parts of who we are.

A Message of Hope and Transformation

Ultimately, Kintsugi offers a message of hope and transformation. No matter how broken or damaged you feel, there's always potential for renewal. By embracing your imperfections and honoring your scars, you can find strength, beauty, and meaning in the midst of adversity. So, delve deeper into the heart of Kintsugi and discover the profound wisdom it holds for your life's journey.

Embracing Vulnerability for Healing and Growth

In a world that often celebrates strength and resilience, vulnerability is often viewed as a weakness. However, as you delve deeper, you begin to see vulnerability in a different light. It becomes a powerful tool for healing and growth, a bridge to deeper connection and self-acceptance.

The Shared Experience of Brokenness

As James Baldwin reflects, "You think your pain and your heartbreak are unprecedented in the history of the world, but then you read." Sharing our vulnerabilities allows us to discover this profound connection with others. We realize, as Baldwin suggests, that our struggles are not unique burdens, but threads woven into the tapestry of human experience.

This shared experience fosters empathy and understanding. We see our "cracks," our vulnerabilities, reflected in others, and this knowledge allows us to heal. It reminds us that we are not alone in our struggles, and that there is strength in acknowledging our vulnerabilities.

The Art of Kintsugi and the Power of Vulnerability

The Japanese art of Kintsugi offers a beautiful metaphor for this concept. Broken pottery is not discarded, but meticulously repaired with precious metals like gold, silver, or platinum. The cracks, instead of being hidden, are celebrated and highlighted. Similarly, by embracing our vulnerabilities, we don't erase our past hurts, but rather fill them with self-compassion, wisdom, and resilience.

Vulnerability as a Catalyst for Growth

Sharing our vulnerabilities also opens the door to personal growth. By confronting our fears and insecurities head-on, we begin to dismantle the walls that have kept us trapped in shame and self-doubt. Vulnerability allows us to be authentic and connect with others on a deeper level. It empowers us to navigate life's challenges with grace and courage.

A Powerful Example: Angelina Jolie's Choice

Consider the story of Angelina Jolie. After undergoing genetic testing and learning she had a significantly elevated risk of developing breast cancer due to a BRCA1 gene mutation, Jolie made a courageous and vulnerable decision. She publicly shared her story and opted for a prophylactic double mastectomy, a preventive measure to take control of her health.

Jolie's act of vulnerability empowered countless women to learn about their own genetic risks and take action for their well-being. It sparked important conversations about preventive healthcare and highlighted the importance of taking control of one's health journey.

This example showcases the power of vulnerability. By openly sharing her story, Jolie not only made a life-saving decision for herself, but also empowered others to prioritize their health and well-being.

VULNERABILITY AND THE POWER OF CREATIVE EXPRESSION

Even creative expression, as Seth Godin highlights in his influential book "V is for Vulnerable," thrives on vulnerability. Godin argues, "Vulnerable is the only way we can feel when we truly share the art we've made. When we share it, when we connect, we have shifted all the power and made ourselves naked in front of the person we've given the gift of our art to."

THE PATH TO WHOLENESS

Embracing vulnerability is a transformative journey—one that requires courage, humility, and self-compassion. As you lean into vulnerability, you discover the power of authenticity and connection, paving the way for greater healing and growth.

POWER TIP

Embrace your vulnerabilities, they are not weaknesses, but badges of courage and resilience on your journey toward wholeness.

CHAPTER 20

Discovering, Crafting, and Sharing Your Story

"There is no greater agony than bearing an untold story inside you." - Maya Angelou

Earlier in the book when we discussed ways to get out of your head, I told you one of the biggest challenges people have is that they don't know how to tell their story.

Now that we've laid the groundwork for understanding your talents, the power of storytelling, and the importance of sharing your unique narrative, let's discuss some practical strategies for discovering, crafting, and sharing your story.

REFLECT ON YOUR JOURNEY

Take some time to reflect on your life experiences, both positive and negative. Consider the significant moments, the turning points, and the lessons you've learned along the way. Journaling can be a helpful tool for this process, allowing you to explore your thoughts and emotions in depth.

IDENTIFY KEY THEMES

Look for recurring themes or motifs in your life story. These could be themes of resilience, perseverance, love, loss, or personal growth. Identifying these themes will help you articulate the core message of your story and convey it more effectively to your audience.

EMBRACE VULNERABILITY

Sharing your story requires a willingness to be vulnerable and authentic. Don't be afraid to share your struggles, fears, and failures alongside your triumphs. Vulnerability fosters connection and empathy, making your story more relatable and impactful.

Find Your Unique Voice

Your voice is what sets your story apart from others. Embrace your unique perspective, personality, and style of storytelling. Whether you're witty, introspective, or passionate, let your authentic voice shine through in your narrative.

Practice Active Listening

Pay attention to the stories of others, both in person and through various forms of media. Listen with empathy and curiosity, seeking to understand different perspectives and experiences. Active listening will not only enrich your own storytelling, but also deepen your connections with others.

Seek Feedback

Share drafts of your story with trusted friends, family members, or mentors for feedback. Their perspectives can offer valuable insights and help you refine your message for maximum impact. Be open to constructive criticism and use it to strengthen your storytelling skills.

Choose Your Medium

Consider the most effective medium for sharing your story. Whether it's through writing, public speaking, podcasting, video, or social media, choose a format that aligns with your strengths and preferences. Experiment with different mediums to find the one that best suits your storytelling style.

Start Small

You don't need to share your entire life story all at once. Start small by sharing snippets of your experiences in everyday conversations, blog posts, or social media updates. Gradually build confidence in sharing more personal and vulnerable aspects of your story over time.

Remember, your story is a powerful tool for connection, inspiration, and personal growth. Embrace the opportunity to share your unique perspective with the world, knowing that your voice matters and has the potential to make a difference in the lives of others.

Overcoming Fear of Resistance

While some individuals naturally find it easy to share their stories, many others grapple with fears and resistance that can hold them back from opening up. Common concerns include the fear of judgment, rejection, or vulnerability. However, with the right strategies and mindset, it's possible to overcome these barriers and build confidence in sharing personal experiences authentically.

For those who have always felt comfortable sharing their stories, like myself, it may be challenging to understand the hesitations others face. However, recognizing that these fears are valid and common is the first step in offering support and guidance to those who need it.

One of the most impactful experiences that helped me build confidence in sharing stories was my background in professional sales. Throughout my career, I've worked in various sales roles, from door-to-door selling to business-to-business sales. The comprehensive sales training provided by top companies equipped me with essential skills, including strategies for quickly building rapport with others.

Sales training often emphasizes the importance of connecting with people on a personal level, understanding their needs, and effectively communicating solutions. These skills are not only invaluable in sales but also in storytelling. By learning how to establish trust and rapport with strangers, I gained the confidence to share my own experiences openly and authentically.

For those looking to overcome fear and resistance in sharing their stories, consider exploring opportunities in sales or seeking out sales training programs. These experiences can provide valuable insights and techniques for building confidence, connecting with others, and effectively sharing personal narratives.

Remember, overcoming fear and resistance is a journey, and it's okay to start small. Celebrate each step forward, and don't hesitate to seek support from friends, mentors, or professional resources along the way. By embracing vulnerability and sharing our stories authentically, we can inspire others and create meaningful connections that resonate deeply.

Power Tip

No one can compete with you at being you. So why try to be someone else?

CHAPTER 21

TIME AND YOUR SUCCESS

"The time is now." - Dr. Martin Luther King, Jr.

Time management is a crucial skill for anyone aiming to achieve their goals. In this chapter, we'll explore the importance of time and delve into practical strategies to make the most of every minute, just like Dr. Martin Luther King Jr. urged us to do with his powerful quote, "The time is now."

I like to think of life as a stage play. In life's play, time takes charge as both the director and the stage itself. It guides how things happen, weaving the past, present, and future together. But in our busy lives, do we ever stop to think about how important time really is? Do we see each moment passing by as a chance to shape our future?

Dr. Martin Luther King Jr., a symbol of hope, knew how crucial the present moment was. He talked about the urgency of now, saying we need to act with determination right away. For him, the time to make a difference wasn't in the future—it was right here, right now, where change starts.

As you dive into understanding the importance of time, remember Dr. King's words. Realize that the present moment is what matters most. It's like a blank canvas where you can create your life, a stage where you can dance to your dreams. But in the beauty of the present, there's also a reminder that life is short and moves quickly.

You're Going To Die

You're going to die, but you don't have to let your dreams die with you. - Rodney Goldston

To truly appreciate the fleeting nature of time, I often take walks in a nearby cemetery. It might seem like an unusual practice, but it serves as a powerful reminder of how time keeps moving forward, no matter what. This cemetery isn't just a place for the dead—it's a place full of potential that was never realized. It's where dreams and ideas are buried with the people who had them.

As I stroll among the graves, I can't help but think about how short life is and how important it is to make the most of our time. Each tombstone tells a story of someone's life and the legacy they left behind. It's a reminder that we all have an expiration date. But in that reminder, there's also a chance for us to do something meaningful with our time—to chase our dreams, to live passionately, and to leave a lasting impact on the world.

MAKE EVERY MINUTE COUNT

One of the speakers who really inspires me is Dr. Willie Jolley. He wrote a book called "It Only Takes a Minute," and he has this powerful message: Every single minute counts if you want to succeed in life. Why? Because a successful life is built on successful minutes.

Think about it like this: If you use each minute well, you can have a successful hour. And if you have successful hours, you can have successful days. Then, successful days lead to successful months, which lead to successful years, and eventually, a successful life. It all starts with just a minute.

There's a poem by Benjamin Mays that captures this idea perfectly. It's called "I Have Only Just a Minute." It talks about how we're given just a minute—sixty seconds—and it's up to us to make the most of it. Even though it seems short, that minute holds the potential for eternity. It's a reminder for all of us to use our time wisely and make every minute count.

Time Management Strategies

Here are some actionable tips to take control of your time and use it effectively.

Set SMART Goals

Specific, Measurable, Achievable, Relevant, and Time-bound goals provide direction and focus for your time investment.

Create a Schedule

Plan your day by allocating time slots for specific tasks. This helps prioritize and avoid procrastination.

Minimize Distractions

Silence notifications, turn off unnecessary apps, and find a quiet workspace to maximize focus during dedicated work periods.

Power Tip
Wasting time is the same as wasting your life.

# CHAPTER 22

THOU SHALL STEAL

"Art is theft." - Pablo Picasso

Successful people throughout history haven't created everything from scratch. Instead, they've learned from and built upon the work of those who came before them. This chapter explores the concept of being inspired by the achievements of others and using their knowledge as a springboard for your own success.

When I taught a series on success to a group of high schoolers, one concept proved particularly challenging for them to grasp: the idea that "good artists copy, great artists steal," as famously stated by Steve Jobs, who echoed Salvador Dali's assertion that "Those who do not want to imitate anything produce nothing." We're often taught from a young age that stealing is wrong, yet we readily accept the notion of not reinventing the wheel. Hip hop music, for instance, was built on the idea of sampling, where artists borrow beats and melodies from existing songs. Notorious B.I.G's "Mo

Pick Yourself For Success

Money Mo Problems" samples Diana Ross's "I'm Coming Out," while Public Enemy's "Fight the Power" draws inspiration from The Isley Brothers' track of the same name.

Let me be abundantly clear, plagiarism is a huge no no. I'm not encouraging you to take the ideas or creations of others and call them your own. I want you to learn to start with the work of others and innovate by adding your own uniqueness. Think of this as furthering the work that someone else has started.

The significance of "stealing" for success lies in the acknowledgment that there's nothing truly original; every creation is influenced by what came before. Instead of shying away from this truth, you should embrace it, allow yourself to be influenced, educated, and inspired by the work of others. Remember what Steve Jobs said, "All great artists steal."

Take, for example, the 1968 footage of the Jackson 5 audition for Motown, where a nine year-old Michael Jackson imitated James Brown. Decades later, at the 2003 BET Awards, Michael Jackson surprised James Brown by presenting him with the Lifetime Achievement Award. This transformation from imitator to influencer is a testament to the power of stealing for success. When James Brown accepted the award, he acknowledged Michael's journey, saying that Michael started by imitating him but then added his own genius to what he had learned from him. This recognition highlights

Rodney Goldston

how learning from and building upon the work of others can lead to remarkable achievements.

Have you ever witnessed the flamboyant Lady Gaga performing on her piano while standing, with one leg extended across the keys? This is a signature move that Little Richard often employed during his live shows, symbolizing his boundless artistic energy that transcended the confines of his seat.

Have you come across an image of Tupac Shakur sporting a scarf tied around his head with a knot in front? This distinctive fashion statement was popularized by none other than Little Richard himself.

Upon Richard's passing, Elton John took to Twitter to express his profound admiration: "Without a doubt — musically, vocally and visually – he was my biggest influence."

It's not an understatement to say that every musical artist that came onto the scene after Little Richard stole something from him.

Similarly, Muhammad Ali's fighting style was inspired by Sugar Ray Robinson, which Bruce Lee then incorporated into his Jeet Kune Do. Dr. Martin Luther King Jr. also drew inspiration from Mahatma Gandhi's principles of nonviolent resistance in his pursuit of civil rights. These examples highlight the transformative power of influence and the ways in which ideas are passed down and reinterpreted across generations.

So, if visionaries like Steve Jobs, Salvador Dali, Elton John, and Muhammad Ali understood the importance of stealing the work of others, why shouldn't you? Remember, stealing, in this context, doesn't mean taking credit for someone else's work or plagiarizing. Instead, it's about honoring those who came before us, giving credit where it's due, and acknowledging that every creation builds upon the foundations laid by those who came before us.

How To Steal Your Way to the Top

1. Always Give Full Credit

2. Don't plagiarize! Always give credit where credit is due.

3. Study the Masters

Dive into the work of those who have achieved greatness in your field. Whether it's reading books, watching interviews, or analyzing their techniques, immerse yourself in their knowledge and experience.

Emulate Success

Identify successful individuals or companies that inspire you and model your approach after theirs. Pay attention to their strategies, habits, and mindset, and adapt them to fit your own goals and aspirations.

Borrow Ideas

Don't be afraid to borrow ideas and concepts from others. Whether it's a marketing strategy, product design, or business model, draw inspiration from a variety of sources and tailor them to suit your unique vision.

Network and Collaborate

Surround yourself with talented and innovative people who can challenge and inspire you. Collaborate on projects, exchange ideas, and learn from each other's strengths and experiences.

Remix and Innovate

Take existing ideas and put your own spin on them. Combine different concepts, experiment with new approaches, and push the boundaries of what's possible. Innovation often comes from building upon what already exists.

Stay Curious

Cultivate a mindset of lifelong learning and curiosity. Stay open to new ideas, perspectives, and opportunities, and never stop seeking knowledge and inspiration from the world around you.

TAKE ACTION

Ultimately, the key to success is taking action. Don't get stuck in analysis paralysis or wait for the perfect moment. Instead, start implementing the ideas and strategies you've learned, and be willing to adapt and iterate as you go.

By embracing the art of stealing, you can leverage the wisdom and insights of those who have come before you to accelerate your own journey to success. So don't be afraid to steal shamelessly, learn voraciously, and create boldly. Your path to greatness awaits.

POWER TIP

Start with the letter M and steal from these people. You can't go wrong. Martin Luther King, Jr., Mandela, Mother Theresa, Mahatma Gandhi, and Muhammad Ali.

CHAPTER 23

THIS MIGHT NOT WORK

"Only those who will risk going too far can possibly find out how far one can go." - T.S. Eliot

Success rarely emerges from playing it safe. Often, the greatest achievements require venturing into the unknown and taking calculated risks that others may shy away from. Guaranteed outcomes can sometimes be a sign that the path you're on might not lead to groundbreaking results. This chapter explores the importance of embracing risk and innovation as you navigate your journey to greatness.

Pick Yourself For Success

Consider the pioneering spirit of Karl Benz, inventor of the automobile in the late 19th century. When Benz created the first car, there were no established roads, and even after its invention, driving was still illegal in many places. Despite these challenges, Benz persevered, recognizing the transformative potential of his invention for transportation and society as a whole. His willingness to embrace risk paved the way for a revolution in mobility.

The reality is, significant progress and meaningful change often require doing something that might not work. Another powerful example of this comes from Procter & Gamble during the Great Depression. While other companies slashed advertising budgets, Procter & Gamble took a bold risk and expanded theirs. They poured resources into radio drama commercials for their soap products, effectively pioneering what we now know as soap operas. This unconventional approach paid off in spades, leading to a significant boost in sales and brand recognition. The lesson here? During times of hardship, sometimes expansion, not contraction, is the key to success.

CALCULATED RISKS, NOT BLIND LEAPS

Throughout history, countless individuals and organizations have thrived by embracing risk and pursuing innovative ideas. Here are a few remarkable examples.

APPLE INC.

Under Steve Jobs' leadership, Apple consistently challenged the status quo with groundbreaking products like the iPhone and iPad. Jobs' willingness to take risks and embrace unconventional approaches propelled Apple to become one of the world's most valuable companies.

NETFLIX

Few could have predicted Netflix's transformation from a DVD rental service to a global streaming powerhouse. By taking calculated risks and investing in original content, Netflix revolutionized the entertainment industry and disrupted traditional media models.

MARIE CURIE

A pioneer in radioactivity research, Curie's groundbreaking discoveries earned her two Nobel Prizes and laid the foundation for modern physics and chemistry. Despite facing significant obstacles as a woman in science, Curie persevered and changed the course of history through her unwavering pursuit of knowledge.

These examples serve as a powerful reminder that greatness often lies on the other side of uncertainty. Embracing calculated risks and pushing the boundaries of what is possible can unlock new opportunities and drive meaningful change. The next time you're faced with a challenge or opportunity, remember: this might not work, but it just might lead to something extraordinary as well.

The Importance of Risk Management

Taking calculated risks doesn't mean being reckless. Successful risk-takers understand the importance of careful assessment. Before taking a leap, consider the potential consequences and create a backup plan if necessary. This doesn't mean every risk will pay off, and that's okay. Learning from both successes and failures is crucial for growth and future endeavors.

Going Not Knowing: A Personal Story

The concept of "going not knowing" perfectly embodies the essence of embracing calculated risks. In some situations, the path forward may not be entirely clear, but we can still make progress by taking a measured leap of faith based on our convictions and careful planning. This is exactly what my wife and I did when we decided to homeschool our daughter, she was in elementary school, and we were both working demanding, full-time corporate jobs. Financially, the situation seemed precarious. We weren't entirely sure how we would make ends meet, yet we firmly believed in the benefits of homeschooling for our daughter. So, we took a leap of faith, embraced the unknown, and committed to "going not knowing."

Through a combination of blessings, hard work, and careful budgeting, we were able to navigate the financial challenges. We never missed a mortgage payment, maintained a modest lifestyle, and even managed to take family vacations. This experience taught us the power of faith, calculated risk-taking and the importance of trusting our convictions even when the path forward isn't entirely clear. If the path is always perfectly clear and risk-free, there's no need for faith or courage. It's venturing into the unknown, trusting your gut, and taking calculated risks that allows you to achieve extraordinary things.

Power Tip

Carefully assess risks and rewards before taking action, but don't let fear of failure paralyze you entirely. Remember, even the most groundbreaking achievements often started with a leap of faith. Sometimes, the greatest breakthroughs come from those who dare to venture beyond the comfort zone and embrace the unknown. So, take a deep breath, trust your instincts, and be willing to take calculated risks as you pursue your dreams.

Pick Yourself For Success

CHAPTER 24

MAKE A DECISION

"It is in your moments of decision that your destiny is shaped" - Tony Robins

But what does it mean to truly make a wise decision? Life is a journey paved with choices, each one an opportunity to shape your path. From seemingly trivial everyday decisions to momentous crossroads, the choices we make hold immense power. But what does it truly mean to make a decision?

The word 'decision' is itself revealing. Derived from the Latin "decidere," it translates to "to cut out." When we make a decision, we're essentially prioritizing one option over another. This doesn't necessarily mean complete elimination, but rather a conscious choice to focus our energy and resources on what matters most.

Prioritizing for Success

As someone who spends a lot of time in the garden, I know firsthand the importance of creating the right conditions for success. To cultivate vibrant flowers, you need to carefully tend to the soil, provide adequate sunlight and water, and sometimes, remove weeds that compete for resources. Similarly, success in life requires prioritizing and nurturing what will help you flourish. This might involve removing negative influences, as discussed in the previous chapter on "Stupid People," such as toxic relationships or unproductive habits. But it goes beyond just removing negativity.

Making Wise Choices

So how do we make wise choices that propel us forward? Here's a simple 3-step framework:

1. Envision the Ideal Outcome

When faced with a decision, close your eyes and imagine the best possible scenario. What excites you most about this potential choice? How does it align with your long-term goals and values? This visualization helps you connect with the motivation behind your decision.

2. Consider the Potential Impact

Be realistic. Every choice has the potential for both positive and negative consequences. What are the potential drawbacks or risks associated with this decision? Are these manageable or outweighed by the potential benefits?

3. Evaluate Your Alignment

Ultimately, can you live with the potential downsides? Does the decision truly resonate with who you are and what you want to achieve? If the answer is yes, proceed with confidence. If not, consider other options or gather more information before making a choice.

So essentially what I'm saying here is consider the best thing that can happen, and the worst thing that can happen. If you can live with the worst possible outcome, consider moving forward.

Leading with Wisdom: Historical Examples

Making wise decisions often involves prioritizing what matters most, even if it goes against the grain. For example, in 2022, at the age of 55, I decided

Pick Yourself For Success

to go back to school to get an MBA. While some might have questioned the logic of pursuing an advanced degree at that stage in my career, the decision aligned perfectly with my long-term goals and desire for continued growth.

History is filled with examples of individuals who made wise choices that shaped the course of events. Here are a few, with a clearer focus on the specific decisions made:

Walt Disney and the Creation of Disneyland: Walt Disney, facing initial skepticism from banks who deemed the project risky, nevertheless cut out the option of playing it safe. He prioritized his vision for a magical theme park experience, meticulously planning every detail and building a supportive network of talented animators and engineers. This decision to prioritize his vision and build a strong team led to the creation of Disneyland, a global entertainment icon.

Yvon Chouinard and Patagonia: Yvon Chouinard, founder of Patagonia, faced a decision: prioritize short-term profits or prioritize environmental responsibility and ethical business practices. He cut out the focus solely on profit margins and prioritized using sustainable materials and fair labor practices. This decision might have seemed risky in a purely profit-driven market, but Patagonia has thrived by building a loyal customer base who value these commitments. Chouinard's decision to prioritize his values has led to a successful and environmentally conscious company.

President John F. Kennedy and the Cuban Missile Crisis: During this tense standoff with the Soviet Union, President Kennedy faced immense pressure to launch a military strike. He cut out the option of immediate military action, prioritizing the need to avoid nuclear war. Instead, he prioritized a diplomatic solution through a naval blockade and back-channel communication. This wise decision to prioritize peace over escalation helped resolve the crisis and potentially prevent a global catastrophe.

These examples showcase how wise decision-making involves prioritizing what matters most, even if it means "cutting out" seemingly easier or more popular options. The act of prioritizing sets these individuals apart and leads to remarkable achievements.

Building a Supportive Network

Wise decision-making involves prioritizing what matters most, as showcased by these examples. Surrounding yourself with positive influences who support your growth, inspire you to be your best self, and share your values is key. Build a network of mentors, friends, and colleagues who uplift and challenge you on your journey. This supportive network acts as a wind beneath your wings, propelling you towards your goals.

CHOOSE WISELY, LIVE INTENTIONALLY

Remember, the choices you make today shape the reality you experience tomorrow. Embrace the power of decision-making and prioritize what truly matters. By following this framework and building a supportive network, you can navigate life's crossroads with confidence and pave the way for a fulfilling and successful future.

POWER TIP

Take some time this week to reflect on a current decision you're facing. Apply the 3-step framework outlined above and consider who in your network might offer valuable insights or support as you move forward with your choice.

CHAPTER 25

WHAT'S YOUR AZIMUTH?

"Do you know where you're going? Do you like the things that life is showing you?" - Diana Ross theme from Mahogany

Growing up I had Diana's album cover for her album Diana tacked to the wall over my bed. If I close my eyes I can hear her beautiful voice singing these lyrics. And so I'm asking you. Do you know where you're going to?

Azimuth is a fancy word for a straight line used in land navigation. Land navigation is a fundamental skill for soldiers in any branch of the military. However, my journey with land navigation began with a series of humbling experiences.

Pick Yourself For Success

As a soldier in the United States Army, I initially found land navigation quite challenging. Picture this: weekend drills where I'd be blindfolded, dropped off in the woods armed with nothing but a map, protractor, compass, and a trusty writing utensil (a military euphemism for a pencil), and instructed to find my way back in time for chow. What's supposed to happen is that you look at your surroundings, take out your map, based on the surroundings you see figure out where you are on the map, identify where you want to be on the map, use your protractor and pencil to draw a straight line from where you are to where you want to be, and use your compass to walk along that azimuth. Unfortunately, I never managed to make it to where I needed to be.

It wasn't until a special forces soldier was brought in to mentor me that I began to grasp the intricacies of land navigation. I learned to discern depressions (or holes in the ground), identify hills and bodies of water, and most crucially, how to shoot an azimuth and stay on course. Through this arduous process, several valuable lessons emerged.

Firstly, recognizing the terrain is essential. To reach your destination, you must intimately understand the landscape surrounding you. Secondly, pinpointing your current location is paramount. Without knowing where you are, it's impossible to chart a path forward. Lastly, the longer you stray from the correct path, even by a single degree, the further you veer from your desired destination.

Rodney Goldston

This lesson extends far beyond the realm of military training—it's a metaphor for life itself. Just as in land navigation, success in life requires a clear understanding of your surroundings, an accurate assessment of your current position, and a steadfast commitment to staying on course. Each decision, each action sets the trajectory for your journey.

In military terms, shooting an azimuth involves selecting a precise direction and following it with unwavering determination. In life and business, this translates to setting clear goals and pursuing them relentlessly. Much like a soldier navigating rugged terrain, shooting an azimuth in life requires focus, resilience, and adaptability.

For example, imagine a business owner aiming to expand their market reach. They must meticulously analyze their current position in the market, identify potential obstacles, and chart a course toward their desired objectives. With a clear azimuth in mind, they can navigate challenges, stay on track, and, ultimately, achieve success.

In essence, knowing your azimuth is about having a clear sense of direction and the determination to stay on course, no matter the obstacles. By applying the principles of land navigation to your life, you can navigate the complexities of existence with purpose, precision, and perseverance.

Power Tip

Just as in land navigation, charting your course by setting clear goals is essential for success in life.

CHAPTER 26

Invest In Yourself

"Never be too poor to pay attention." - Rodney Goldston

I'm constantly amazed when I meet people and they express their aspirations and dreams, but then shy away from investing in their own personal development. They'll tell me they don't have the money for an online course or the time to read a book. Yet, if someone aspired to become a professional athlete, actor, singer, or dancer, they wouldn't think twice about hiring a coach to guide them. It's intuitive to recognize that those who excel in their fields often have personal coaches.

Pick Yourself For Success

Michael Jordan and Kobe Bryant, two of the greatest basketball players of all time, both relied on Tim Grover as their personal coach. The lesson here is clear: never be too poor to pay attention. If you truly want to achieve your dreams, you must invest in yourself.

Let's appeal to logic for a moment. Imagine you could identify a coach who could help you get just one step closer to your goal or dream. What would that be worth to you? It's important to quantify the value of your dream because, as Clarence Avant says, everything boils down to money. When deciding whether to invest in coaching, you need to have a clear understanding of the monetary value of your dream, either to yourself or to the people you seek to impact.

Once you know the value of your dream, ask yourself a simple question: Can this coach, this book, this course get me just 1% closer to my dream, my goal?

Years ago, I invested $3,500 in a marketing certification through HubSpot. While the course was extensive, it was a single lesson on pricing that proved to be invaluable. I applied what I learned and generated $356,000 in revenue. When faced with the cost of coaching or personal development programs, reflect on this potential return on investment.

And let's not forget one of the most cost-effective ways to invest in yourself: reading books. When you read a book, you're essentially getting one-n-one coaching from the author. I vividly remember visiting the legendary Prince's house, where I noticed a huge pile of books in his office. On top of all the books he was actively reading was a Bible, symbolizing that scripture was the final reference for all the information he took in.

Earlier, we discussed the importance of believing that your dream is possible. Matthew 6:21 reminds us, "For where your treasure is, there will your heart be also." If you truly believe in your dream, then investing in yourself becomes a natural extension of that belief. Conversely, a reluctance to invest in yourself may indicate a lack of faith in your potential.

Remember, your dreams are worth investing in. By committing to your personal development, you're not only investing in yourself but also in the realization of your dreams. So, don't hesitate to take that leap and bet on yourself. The dividends of your investment may exceed your wildest expectations.

Practical Ways to Invest in Yourself

Online Courses

Explore reputable online platforms offering courses relevant to your goals and interests. Many platforms offer free or affordable courses on a wide range of topics, allowing you to learn at your own pace and schedule.

BOOKS

Make reading a priority in your life. Invest in books that align with your aspirations and interests. Whether it's self-help, business, or personal development, books provide valuable insights and knowledge to help you grow.

COACHING AND MENTORSHIP

Consider hiring a coach or mentor who can provide personalized guidance and support. A coach can offer valuable feedback, accountability, and strategies to help you overcome obstacles and achieve your goals. [Visit my website](#) for information about my coaching, and mastermind programs.

NETWORKING EVENTS AND WORKSHOPS

Attend networking events, workshops, and seminars relevant to your field or interests. These events provide opportunities to learn from experts, connect with like-minded individuals, and expand your knowledge and skills.

PERSONAL REFLECTION AND GROWTH

Set aside time for self-reflection and personal growth. Journaling, meditation, and goal setting are powerful tools for self-discovery and development. Invest in activities that nurture your mental, emotional, and spiritual well-being.

HEALTH AND WELLNESS

Prioritize your physical health and well-being. Invest in activities that promote fitness, nutrition, and overall wellness, such as exercise classes, healthy cooking lessons, and wellness retreats.

By investing in yourself, you're making a commitment to your personal and professional growth. Remember, the greatest investment you can make is in yourself.

POWER TIP

The more you invest in yourself, the greater the returns you'll reap in both personal and professional fulfillment.

Pick Yourself For Success

CHAPTER 27

OUTWORK EVERYBODY

"When you've exhausted all possibilities remember you haven't" - *Thomas Edison*

In the pursuit of greatness, there's no substitute for hard work and relentless determination. This chapter is dedicated to the importance of cultivating an iconic work ethic that sets you apart from the rest.

As the saying goes, "Hard work outworks talent when talent won't work." This sentiment is exemplified by the remarkable achievements of individuals who have achieved extraordinary success through sheer grit and perseverance.

Pick Yourself For Success

Take Thomas Edison, for example. A renowned inventor and entrepreneur, Edison is best known for inventing the phonograph, motion picture camera, and, most famously, the electric light bulb. Despite facing numerous setbacks and failures, Edison remained undeterred in his pursuit of innovation. It's often said that it took him over a thousand attempts to develop a working light bulb, but Edison famously remarked, "When you think you've exhausted all options, remember you haven't." His unwavering determination and tireless work ethic ultimately led to his groundbreaking inventions that transformed the world.

Similarly, the creators of WD-40, a widely used lubricant and rust-preventative product, encountered numerous obstacles in their quest to develop the perfect formula. The "40" in WD-40 stands for the number of attempts it took to get the formula just right. This serves as a powerful reminder that success often requires persistence and resilience in the face of adversity.

One modern-day example of extraordinary work ethic is Tyler Perry, the most successful African American film director in history. Perry's rise to prominence is a testament to his relentless drive and dedication to his craft. Despite facing countless challenges and setbacks early in his career, Perry refused to give up on his dreams. In the documentary "Maxine's Baby," Perry spoke about his unwavering commitment to outworking everyone else. While he acknowledges that there may be other directors more talented than he is, Perry's relentless work ethic sets him apart from the competition.

Another illustration of iconic work ethic is found in the legendary basketball player Michael Jordan. Tim Grover, Jordan's longtime trainer, described Jordan's insatiable hunger for improvement, even after winning championships. Jordan understood that success is fleeting and that to stay on top, he had to continually push himself to new heights. This mindset of relentless pursuit of excellence propelled Jordan to become one of the greatest athletes of all time.

So, how can you cultivate an iconic work ethic that propels you toward personal and professional success? Here are a few tips.

1. Set Clear Goals

Define what success looks like for you and create a roadmap to achieve your objectives.

2. Prioritize Tasks

Focus on high-impact activities that move you closer to your goals and avoid distractions.

3. Embrace Challenges

View obstacles as opportunities for growth and learning, and tackle them head-on with determination.

4. Stay Disciplined

Develop habits and routines that support your goals, and hold yourself accountable for your actions.

5. Keep Learning:

Continuously seek out opportunities to expand your knowledge and skills, and never stop striving for improvement.

By adopting these principles and committing to outworking everyone else, you can unlock your full potential and achieve greatness in every aspect of your life. Remember, success is not determined by talent alone but by the relentless pursuit of excellence through hard work and perseverance.

Power Tip

Start your day with intention. Take a few minutes each morning to prioritize your tasks and set realistic goals for what you want to accomplish.

CHAPTER 28

BEYOND THE FILTERED LENS

"Comparison is the thief of your joy." - Rodney Goldston

In the age of curated online personas, it's easy to fall victim to the age-old adage, "the grass is always greener on the other side of the fence." Picking yourself for success, however, requires a different perspective. This chapter grapples with the comparison trap fueled by social media and offers strategies to cultivate self-belief and satisfaction on your own unique journey.

Pick Yourself For Success

We are bombarded daily with a carefully crafted digital narrative. Scrolling through social media feeds, we encounter a relentless stream of seemingly idyllic vacations, overflowing bank accounts, and picture-perfect relationships. These glimpses into others' lives, however, are meticulously curated for maximum impact. The photos are filtered, the vacations sponsored, and the happiness meticulously staged. This constant exposure to an idealized version of reality can trigger a primal response within us – the desire to keep up with everyone else. Our lizard brain becomes activated, leading to feelings of inadequacy and frustration.

This comparison game can be particularly detrimental to our sense of accomplishment and self-worth. We begin to disregard the strides we've made, the mountains we've climbed, and the battles we've won. The relentless focus on what others possess cultivates jealousy, apathy, and a sense of stagnation.

The key to breaking free from this cycle of comparison lies in understanding the illusion at play. Social media platforms are not a reflection of reality, but rather a highlight reel. We see the celebratory moments, the carefully chosen snapshots, but not the behind-the-scenes struggles, the sacrifices made, or the hidden demons everyone faces. The seemingly perfect lives we envy may harbor their own set of challenges and anxieties, burdens unseen in the filtered photos.

How to Cultivate Self-Belief and Satisfaction Despite the Comparison Trap

Reframe Your Perception

Recognize that social media feeds are a curated narrative, not a documentary. The lives you see online are just one small, staged slice of someone else's journey.

Honor Your Process

Every individual path is unique. Focus on your own growth and celebrate the progress you've made. What struggles have you overcome? What skills have you developed? Take pride in your journey, not just the destination.

Embrace Your Wins

Recognize and celebrate your accomplishments, big or small. Did you finally master that challenging recipe? Did you land that promotion you worked tirelessly for? Acknowledge your successes and allow yourself to feel the satisfaction they bring.

CRAFT YOUR OWN SCOREBOARD

Define success on your terms, not the metrics social media promotes. What truly brings you joy? Is it freedom, meaningful relationships, good health, or the pursuit of a passion? Focus on cultivating the elements that make your life fulfilling, not the number of followers you have, or the size of your bank account.

PRACTICE GRATITUDE

Shift your focus from what you lack to what you already possess. Take time each day to appreciate the blessings in your life – your loved ones, your health, the small moments of joy. Gratitude fosters a sense of contentment and helps to break the cycle of comparison.

Ultimately, picking yourself for success means embracing your own journey and celebrating your unique story. Instead of envying the filtered lives you see online, focus on nurturing your own garden. Water it with self-compassion, fertilize it with gratitude, and cultivate the seeds of your dreams. Remember, the grass may seem greener on the other side, but with dedication and self-belief, you can make your own patch flourish.

CHAPTER 29

CONCLUSION AND NEXT STEPS

Congratulations on completing "Pick Yourself For Success"! This journey we've taken together is a testament to your commitment to growth and self-discovery. Remember, the one thing that you have that nobody else has is you. Your voice, your point of view, your mind, your experiences, your vision, your calling. By engaging with this book, you've taken a significant step in understanding and harnessing your unique greatness.

Pick Yourself For Success

But please remember, this isn't the end—it's a powerful beginning. The strategies you've learned, from ignoring "Stupid People" to "Elevating Your Mind," are tools for a lifetime of growth. Now, it's time to put them into action.

Measure Your Growth with the Greatness Gauge™

Remember the Greatness Gauge you took at the start of our journey? It's time to take it again. Visit www.RodneyGoldston.com/greatness-gauge and retake the assessment. Here's why:

1. **Track Your Progress:** See how your Greatness Profile has evolved. This tangible evidence of your growth will fuel your motivation.

2. **Refine Your Focus:** Your new results will highlight areas where you've excelled and where you still need work, guiding your next steps.

3. **Celebrate Wins**: Every improvement, no matter how small, is a victory. Celebrate these wins—they're proof that you're picking yourself for success.

Share Your Success

Has this book and the Greatness Gauge helped you? Your story could be the spark that ignites someone else's journey. Visit the website where you purchased this book and leave a review. Consider sharing your before and ter Greatness Profiles (if you're comfortable) to show the real impact of his work.

Deepen Your Transformation

- **Join the Pick Yourself For Success Challenge:** For just $97 (General Admission) or $297 (VIP Experience), immerse yourself in this 5-day event. You'll get actionable guidance, accountability, and a community of like-minded achievers. Visit www.RodneyGoldston.com to register.

- **Access the High-Level Mastermind:** Ready to skyrocket your success? Join my exclusive mastermind. Network with top performers, get personalized mentoring, and access resources that turn your Greatness Profile into reality.

- **Stay Connected:** Follow me on social media regular insights, Greatness Gauge updates, and first access to new resources.

A Personal Note

Your decision to pick up this book was the first step in picking yourself for success. By engaging with the SUCCESS system and the Greatness Gauge, you've equipped yourself with potent tools for a life of achievement and fulfillment.

Pick Yourself For Success

But tools are just the beginning. It's your commitment to use them, to continually gauge and grow your greatness, that will make all the difference

So, take the Greatness Gauge again. Join the challenge. Surround yourself with greatness in the mastermind. Your extraordinary life is unfolding, and I'm deeply honored to be part of your journey.

Your greatness is not just a possibility—it's your destiny. Let's bring it to life, one gauged step at a time.

Rodney Goldston

PY4S ZONE

PY4S ZONE
Know your purpose, Overcome obstacles
Live your dreams, Live a life of service,
You outwork everyone, You're comfortable being uncomfortable,
and uncommon

LEARNING ZONE
You start to walk by FAITH, Learn new skills,
You begin to apply "If", "Invictous", and Kintsugi

FEAR ZONE
Live your FEAR's,
Other people's opinions matter,
You make excuses

COMFORT ZONE
You feel safe and,
comfortable.
You take few,
or no risk

©2024 Rodney Goldston

Pick Yourself For Success

ABOUT THE AUTHOR

Rodney Goldston, MBA, is a leading voice in the field of personal development, uniquely blending cutting-edge neuroscience, empirical research, and timeless Biblical wisdom to help individuals achieve their greatest potential. As the architect of the innovative SUCCESS system, Goldston empowers people to overcome self-doubt, build powerful personal brands, and step into their greatness.

His approach, which he calls "The Science and Spirit of Greatness," has helped professionals, entrepreneurs, and individuals from all walks of life elevate their minds and transform their lives. Goldston's teachings are grounded in the latest findings from behavioral science and neuroscience, yet deeply rooted in spiritual principles, offering a holistic path to success and fulfillment.

In his groundbreaking book, "Pick Yourself For Success: How To Step Out Of Your Head And Into Your Greatness," Goldston distills his expertise into actionable strategies. Whether it's understanding the importance of personal branding in the digital age, confronting challenges, or harnessing the power of physical exercise for cognitive enhancement, Goldston's SUCCESS system provides a roadmap for anyone seeking to unlock their full potential.

A dynamic speaker and thought leader, Goldston brings energy, insight, and compassion to his work, inspiring audiences to not just dream of success, but to actively pick themselves to achieve it. With "Pick Yourself For Success," he invites readers on a transformative journey to discover the greatness within themselves.

END NOTES

REFERENCES

CHAPTER 1

Covey, S. R. (1997). The Seven Habits of Highly Effective People: Restoring the Character Ethic. Macmillan Reference USA.

Golding, W. (2003). Lord of the Flies. Penguin.

Haldar, S. (2016). William Golding's Lord of the Flies. Atlantic Publishers & Dist.

Scaltsas, T., & Mason, A. S. (2010). The Philosophy of Epictetus. OUP Oxford.

The Wellness Society. (2024, February 15). Deep Dive: What causes Free-Floating Anxiety? - The Wellness Society | Self-Help, Therapy and

Coaching Tools. The Wellness Society | Self-Help, Therapy and Coaching Tools. https://thewellnesssociety.org/what-causes-free-floating-anxiety/

CHAPTER 2

Personal branding in the age of Google. (2020, December 17). Seth's Blog. https://seths.blog/2009/02/personal-branding-in-the-age-of-google/

I am not a brand. (2020, December 17). Seth's Blog. https://seths.blog/2016/04/i-am-not-a-brand/

CHAPTER 3

Sinek, S. (2011). Start with why: The Inspiring Million-Copy Bestseller That Will Help You Find Your Purpose. Penguin UK.

CHAPTER 4

Duckworth, A. (2016). Grit: The Power of Passion and Perseverance. Random House.

CHAPTER 5

Grinde B (2022) Understanding Free Will as a Biological Phenomenon. Ann Cogn Sci 6(1):211-216

Torres, E., & Fajardo-Chica, D. (2013). Gregg D. Caruso: Free Will and Consciousness: A Determinist account of the illusion of free will. Minds and Machines, 23(4), 519–522. https://doi.org/10.1007/s11023-013-9315-5

Mph, M. T. M. (2020, February 19). Five healthy habits net more healthy years. Harvard Health. https://www.health.harvard.edu/blog/five-healthy-habits-net-more-healthy-years-2020021918907

Chapter 6

King, M. L., Jr. (2024). I've been to the mountaintop. HarperCollins.

Steven Pressfield. (2013, November 4). Writing Wednesdays: Resistance and Self-Loathing. Steven Pressfield | Website of Author and Historian, Steven Pressfield. https://stevenpressfield.com/2013/11/resistance-and-self-loathing/

Professional, C. C. M. (n.d.). Amygdala. Cleveland Clinic. https://my.clevelandclinic.org/health/body/24894-amygdala

Chapter 7

Ratey, J., & Hagerman, E. (2009). Spark!: How Exercise Will Improve the Performance of Your Brain.

What we can all learn from Bob Harper's shocking heart attack. (2018, February 7). NBC News. https://www.nbcnews.com/better/health/what-every-single-person-needs-know-about-heart-health-ncna844881

CHAPTER 9

Rydell, R. J., Rydell, M. T., & Boucher, K. L. (2010). The effect of negative performance stereotypes on learning. Journal of Personality and Social Psychology, 99(6), 883–896. https://doi.org/10.1037/a0021139

CHAPTER 10

Clear, J. (2020, February 3). The domino effect: How to create a chain reaction of good habits. James Clear. https://jamesclear.com/domino-effect

CHAPTER 11

Clear, J. (2020, February 3). The domino effect: How to create a chain reaction of good habits. James Clear. https://jamesclear.com/domino-effect

CHAPTER 13

Mednick, S. C., & Ehrman, M. (2006). Take a nap!: Change Your Life. Workman Publishing.

Chapter 15

Cmaadmin, J. M. B. (2008, June 17). Andrew Carnegie and Race. Diverse: Issues in Higher Education. https://www.diverseeducation.com/institutions/hbcus/article/15087288/andrew-carnegie-and-race

Chapter 16

Ziglar, Z. (2010). See you at the top. Pelican Publishing.

Chapter 18

Gardner, H. E. (2008). Multiple intelligences: New Horizons in Theory and Practice. Hachette UK.

Chapter 19

Manzella, K. P. (n.d.). Kintsugi – Art of Repair | Traditional Kyoto. https://traditionalkyoto.com/culture/kintsugi/

The Angelina Jolie effect: One year later. (2014, May 14). Fred Hutch. https://www.fredhutch.org/en/news/center-news/2014/05/the-angelina-jolie-effect--one-year-later.html

Chapter 21

Jolley, W. (1997). It only takes a minute to change your life.

Chapter 22

Kleon, A. (2012). Steal like an artist: 10 Things Nobody Told You About Being Creative. Hachette UK.

Chapter 26

Grover, T. S., & Wenk, S. (2014). Relentless: From Good to Great to Unstoppable. Simon and Schuster.

Chapter 27

Bekele, Gelila, and Armani Ortiz. Maxine's Baby: The Tyler Perry Story. Dir. Bekele and Ortiz. 2023. Documentary.

Grover, T. S., & Wenk, S. (2014). Relentless: From Good to Great to Unstoppable. Simon and Schuster.